Your Opportunity for a Better Life

Your Opportunity for a *Better* Life

9 Keys To Unlock Success
In Your Life

Jeff Daws
with Chesnee Dorsey

Edited by Joe Oliver

XULON PRESS

Xulon Press
2301 Lucien Way #415
Maitland, FL 32751
407.339.4217
www.xulonpress.com

© 2019 by Jeff Daws

Unless otherwise indicated, Scripture quotations taken from the Holy Bible, New International Version (NIV). Copyright © 1973, 1978, 1984, 2011 by Biblica, Inc.™. Used by permission. All rights reserved.

Scripture quotations taken from the King James Version (KJV) – public domain.

Scripture quotations marked (NKJV) are taken from the New King James Version®. Copyright © 1982 by Thomas Nelson. Used by permission. All rights reserved.

Scripture quotations taken from the Holy Bible, New Living Translation (NLT). Copyright ©1996, 2004, 2007 by Tyndale House Foundation. Used by permission of Tyndale House Publishers, Inc.

Scripture quotations taken from the Contemporary English Version (CEV). Copyright © 1995 American Bible Society. Used by permission. All rights reserved.

Scripture quotations marked (GNT) are from the Good News Translation in Today's English Version- Second Edition Copyright © 1992 by American Bible Society. Used by Permission.

Scripture quotations marked (MSG) are taken from THE MESSAGE, copyright © 1993, 2002, 2018 by Eugene H. Peterson. Used by permission of NavPress. All rights reserved. Represented by Tyndale House Publishers, Inc.

Scripture quotations marked (TLB) are taken from The Living Bible copyright © 1971. Used by permission of Tyndale House Publishers, Inc., Carol Stream, Illinois 60188. All rights reserved.

Scripture quotations marked (ESV) are from the ESV® Bible (The Holy Bible, English Standard Version®), copyright © 2001 by Crossway, a publishing ministry of Good News Publishers. Used by permission. All rights reserved.

Printed in the United States of America.

ISBN-13: 978-1-5456-7528-1

CONTENTS

Dedication

I dedicate this book to my parents and stepparents, who taught me that no matter how hard life becomes, you never give up. To my children, Tyler and Katelyn, I love you both so much. You both are the greatest blessing God gave your mother and me. To my wife, Rhonda, who is the love of my life and the person who believed in me when I didn't believe in myself. I love you, Rhonda! To my staff at the church, thank you for giving your lives to help me fulfill God's vision for our church. To the people of Stockbridge Community Church, for allowing me the privilege to speak into your lives on a weekly basis and for loving my family and me. And to Emily Frisone, who by her courageous fight against cancer, inspired the title of this book.

Chapter 1

Opportunity for a Better Life

*H*ow's your life going right now? Really. How *is* your life going? Is it what you want it to be like? Is it what you envisioned it would be like when you were younger? Maybe you feel like you're on top of the world right now. If that's so, I'm extremely happy for you! But if you're like most people, you probably either responded that your life feels like a boring set of routines that you go through day after day or, worse, that you feel like your life is out of control, overwhelming, and hopeless. If either of these statements describes your life, I want to share with you this good news: your life *can* get better! There is an *opportunity for a better life* through Jesus Christ available to you. There is hope!

So after reading that, you may say to me, "Well, yeah, Jeff, that sounds all great coming from you, but you're a preacher. You work in a church. You look like you've got it all together. What do you know about life's challenges? What do you know about pain? What do you know about failure?"

Well, my friend, those are good questions, especially since you may have only seen me on a Sunday morning when I was speaking to a crowd or in a video that's been edited. That *is* me on stage and in the videos,

1

but that is only one part of me. And if you think I'm successful and have it all together, you might be surprised to find out that success is a choice I have to make every day. It's a decision that I have to fight for every morning and that I must continue choosing until I go to sleep that night. In fact, if you knew me years ago, you never would've thought I'd become the person that I am now.

You see, from my beginning, life seemed to be stacked against me.

My parents married when my dad was 18, and my mom was 16. Just after marrying, my mom became pregnant with my brother Jody, and a year and a half after Jody's birth, I was born. I wish I could say I was born into a happy family—that's what I wished for over and over as a child—but unfortunately, my parents were very young, very different, and fought a lot.

Suitcase Kid

Only two years after I was born, my parents divorced, and my brother and I became like so many other modern children have become: every-other-weekend, suitcase kids.

Every other weekend, my brother and I would load up our suitcases with clothes and whatever we needed for the time, piled into the car, and were shipped off to Dad's. I hated this routine of ping-ponging between parents. I felt sad, confused, and pinned between having to choose the love of one parent over another. It's an awful situation for a child to be in, and to think that right now, children all over the world are experiencing this same type of hell fills me with sadness.

Perhaps you experienced something similar when you were a child.

To say that divorce is difficult on children is an understatement. Children do not have the life-experience needed to help them adjust to such huge, sudden changes in family life. Children are not emotionally or psychologically prepared for the earthquake of divorce. Their lives are literally shaken to the core.

What happens to these children later in life? Julia Lewis, a professor at San Francisco State University, was curious about the effects of divorce on children and spent 25 years studying and following up with the same group of children of divorced parents. What she found is alarming: *Half* the children became involved in drug and alcohol abuse before they were 14 years old!

According to those stats, it's a miracle that I didn't become a drug addict or alcoholic, and I give praise and thanks to God for that! Had that happened, I have no clue where I would be right now or if I'd even be alive.

But as a child, my life continued on, and I thought, "Nothing could be worse than my parents' divorce."

Oh, how wrong I was.

Childhood Horror

When I was 6, my mother and father both remarried. Unfortunately, my mother's second choice in a spouse was terrible. My new stepfather liked to drink and didn't like to work. His unwillingness to hold a steady job forced my mom to work hard to support us. My mom struggled with balancing the long hours each week that her job demanded with still having to care for two kids and a husband.

And then my mom became pregnant with a third child, putting even more strain on our family. Our finances were a mess, and to survive, we had to move a lot. Sometimes we would move in with my stepfather's parents. They were very nice people and always made me feel good even though I knew they were not my biological grandparents. The other grandkids called this grandfather "Papa Thomas," so that's what I called him as well. Papa Thomas always tried to help my family when his son refused to work or went off on a drinking binge.

Despite the pain of being partially separated from my real father and being shuffled around to other places, an even worse tragedy occurred that same year that has forever haunted my mind. We'd moved into a house in a small town called Social Circle, Georgia, that was not too far from Papa Thomas—most likely he paid the rent on it.

One December day, my brother—only a year and a half older than me—started feeling very ill. He was showing signs of the flu, and so Mom took him to one of the town's doctors. After examination, the doctor didn't notice anything unusual other than cold/flu symptoms we'd seen. He sent my brother home with the encouraging news that my brother would be fine in a couple of days. When we got home, my brother rallied some, and he and I played together. Despite my brother being sick, we were both excited because Christmas was just a few days away.

Early December 24, I was sleeping on the bottom bunk of my bunk bed when I was jarred awake by the sound of my mother's voice screaming for me. I jumped out of bed and ran into the small living room to see my mom over the top of my brother. To my horror, my brother was convulsing violently on the floor. My mom had inserted a spoon into his mouth to prevent him from biting his tongue. Frantic, Mom yelled for me to get help from our next-door neighbors since we didn't have a phone in our house. I hurried as fast as I could to the neighbor's house, banging on their door until they answered.

The rest of the day was a blurred nightmare, but when it ended, my brother—my best friend—was dead. We'd learn later that he didn't have the flu but an even more dangerous viral infection called spinal meningitis.

Instead of being a time of celebration, that Christmas became a time of shock, grief, and mourning. I can remember going to the funeral home and seeing my brother lying in his little casket, wearing his gray suit—his only suit. At that moment, I felt numb. I remember riding in my grandmother's car. She had an eight-track tape player and was playing a song by Charlie Pride called "Snakes Crawl at Night." The whole moment felt so eerie. We've all had dreams that we've woken up from and sighed with relief, "Thank God it was just a dream." Well, this was a nightmare I wanted to wake up from, but I couldn't because it was my new reality.

All of this experience was awful, and I wouldn't wish it on anyone. As an adult looking back on my life, I knew that Romans 8:28 (NIV) proclaims, "And we know that in all things God works for the good of those who love him." I believe that this verse is true, so I chose to look deep into this pit of sadness for some ray of light, some beacon of hope, something—anything—good that came of this tragedy. And I found something!

Glimmer of Hope

Around this time, my dad had just started going to church. He had remarried rather quickly after the divorce, and he and my stepmother started attending a small Church of God in Monroe, Georgia. When my brother died, the people in that church showed me a love that would impact my dad in a big way. They collected money and food for our family, and they did all they could to help us. My dad and stepmother became followers of Jesus, and their life-changing decision would begin to be their *opportunity for a better life.* The love of God was shown to my dad during the most tragic time in his life. Though at the time, it seemed like God was a mile away, I believe that God was with my family before, during, and after this tragedy. No matter what tragic, disturbing, or sorrowful turns our lives take, God can take the worst of things and use them to bring out the best in people.

My dad and stepmother became regular attenders of their church and have remained there for over forty years—something which has been a great benefit to their lives over the decades.

As for me, back when I was 6, I had a difficult time adjusting to my brother's absence. Despite now being surrounded by children, with my stepmother having two children—a son who was three years older than me and a daughter my same age—I still thought of my brother when I packed my suitcase every other weekend to stay with Dad.

But more children kept coming. My father and stepmother had two more children together, bringing our total to five. Then, my mother and her second husband had two more children, twins! Now there were four children at my mom's. It felt like there were children everywhere. But where did I fit in? I felt somewhat lost in this sea of kids. I can't even imagine what my mom was going through at this time.

With four kids and having to work even harder to support her family and somehow manage to hold her marriage together, she carried a huge weight on her shoulders. But a terrible cycle developed between her and my stepfather. Their disagreements would explode, and I remember watching them fight, sometimes physically. Around this time, I began to develop issues of my own that would affect me for a long time.

As my mom did all she could to provide for our family while my stepdad did nothing but make empty promises to get better, I angrily watched from the sideline, desperately wanting things to change for the better but unable as a child to do anything about our situation. I remember wanting him to go away and never come back. One time, my mom said that my stepdad was not coming back, and I felt so happy that he would finally be out of our house. But a few weeks later, he showed up again, and I felt disappointed beyond words.

Finally, after more of this back and forth, my mom had enough. I don't know what happened between them to prompt my mom's final decision, but she took action in a dramatic way. At the time, we were living in a small trailer park with about 10 homes. Our trailer sat beside a big barrel where neighbors burned their trash. With fury, Mom took all of my stepdad's clothes, put them in the trash barrel, and burned them! That was the beginning of things getting better for us.

No longer able to stay in the trailer, we moved in with my mom's parents. They lived in a very small two-bedroom house, which was a tight fit for my grandparents, their youngest son, my mom, and her four children. Nevertheless, my grandparents always did whatever they could to help out their children and grandchildren with what they needed. Somehow, with only two beds in each bedroom and a sofa bed in the living room, we all managed to sleep each night. I never realized how small that house was until I went back and visited it as an adult.

This was a pivotal time in my mom's life. Pulling from inner strength, she decided she was going to make it on her own. Because Mom only completed up to the 7th grade in school, her job prospects were limited, particularly to labor-intensive work. But she got a job with a company in our town that made plastic products, like 2-liter bottles for soft drinks. The work was hard and required long hours, but the income allowed her to move us into our own rental house when I was about 10 years old. The house was located in a "mill village"—a cluster of small houses built near a cotton mill to give the workers a place to live close to work. It wasn't the best area of town, but we were close to my grandparents.

As time moved on, Mom worked hard and received promotions at the factory, eventually learning how to operate and fix the machines in the factory. She was one of the few women at the time who could do this kind of work, but she had determined within her heart to do whatever it took to improve our living situation.

With my mom at work for most of the day, you may be wondering who took care of my little brother and sister. Yep, that's right; I did. At the time, I was 10 years old and never would've thought that I'd be a pastor later on in life. But it was during this season of caring for my siblings that I started to learn how to care for and lead people.

On every other weekend, I was still packing my suitcase and going to my dad's house. Dad almost always arrived promptly to pick me up. I always looked forward to going to his house. Since my dad had remarried and become a Christian, it became apparent to me that God was blessing him. Dad now lived in a new house that he and his wife kept very tidy and clean. Their house was like a different world from any of the rundown, falling apart places that my mom and stepdad rented. Visiting Dad's place was such a drastic difference in living from the poverty I was used to. Even though Dad was lower middle class, I thought he was rich! Like Mom, Dad was a hard worker, typically working two jobs to provide for his family. He was a small engine mechanic, which to me at the time meant that he worked on lawnmowers. Now I understand that he did so much more.

But no matter how much I enjoyed spending time at Dad's, I always had to repack my suitcase at the end of the weekend to go back to Mom's. I remember thinking I really didn't fit in with either of my parents or my siblings: I was the half-brother and the stepbrother. After my only real brother died, I felt like a "part-time child." I started to feel like I was the outsider in my own family. Divorce is terribly hard for children.

I was very unhappy. And through all of this turmoil, a strong desire to fit in started to grow within me.

Goodbye South

My mom remarried again, and the third time was a charm. My new stepfather was a good man who worked and liked to play basketball and baseball with my siblings and me. Right after they got married, my stepfather got a job offer in Worcester, Massachusetts, so we moved over 1,000 miles away, leaving behind the small country town of Monroe, Georgia. But more importantly, to me later, I would now be living far away from my father.

In the beginning, the new location was fun. We moved to a house that was on a small lake, where there were a lot of kids who were around my age. I made many friends quickly, and because it was summer, I spent a good deal of time fishing—what more could a country boy from Georgia want? Unfortunately, the summer fishing season didn't last long. Compared to Georgia, it got cold very quickly and eventually much colder than I had ever experienced! Soon, the lake froze over, and the kids who lived around the lake played out on the ice. At first, my mom was hesitant to let us join them on the ice since it rarely gets cold enough in Georgia to freeze the surface of a lake. But the other parents assured her that the ice was safe.

That was a winter I will never forget. It snowed and snowed and snowed. Sometimes, a foot of snow would fall overnight. In Georgia, if it snowed an inch, everything shut down, but that was not the case in Massachusetts. So, I was amazed by the snowfall.

I also remember riding the school bus for the first time. The middle school and the high school were all in the same location. The first day I got on the school bus I was shocked that it had a radio on it and speakers blaring heavy metal music. The driver seemed to not care about what was happening around him, and he certainly could not hear what was going on because the music was so loud. This was really different from the Georgia school bus drivers who assigned me to a seat.

Though I can't say for certain, it appeared to me at the time that my new bus driver was crazy. Despite snow covering the roads, he didn't slow down at all! I can remember being scared at how fast he would drive as the bus slipped and slid over the snow-packed road. One time, we were pulling into our school's icy parking lot, and as we went around the corner, our bus slid out of control, hit the curb next to the sidewalk, and lifted partially off the ground on its side, almost tipping over! Talk about a dramatic entrance!

In school, you would've thought I was from another planet because the other kids would stop me in the hallways and ask me to talk. They had never heard someone speak with a Southern accent and were fascinated by it. But surprisingly to me, it wasn't long before I picked up a New England accent. This first year in Massachusetts turned into a fun one. I had many new experiences, and with the lake frozen, I got to play in the snow and on the ice with all of my new friends who lived around the lake all winter long.

My mother was expecting another baby when we moved up to Massachusetts, and when I was 13, I had a new baby sister. After Mom recovered from having my half-sister, she went back to work. She and my stepdad worked at the same company, so being the oldest brother, I was responsible for taking care of my younger siblings, except for the baby. Because I rode a different bus than my brothers and sister, I got home first, and it was also my responsibility to make sure that the chores were completed around our house. This is where some of my leadership skills started to develop. I delegated chores to my brothers and sister to help me finish our task list before Mom got home. If we didn't finish the daily chores before Mom got home, we knew that we'd be in big trouble! So I made sure that we all got the housework done.

My new stepfather was and is a good man, and I would learn to appreciate him more after I grew up. But during this time, I thought he was just a person who was trying to take my father's place. I hated it when he corrected me or tried to give me guidance. Since he wasn't my biological father, I didn't feel like he had a right to tell me what to do. Finally, I became so irritated with my stepfather, I begged to live with my real dad. And in that spring, when I turned 14, I moved back to Georgia to live with my dad. I dreamed of what it would be like to live with my father again.

At this point in time, there were 3 children already living with my father—my stepmother's daughter and the 2 children my father and stepmother had together. I remember getting on the plane to fly to Georgia and being afraid and excited about air travel at the same time. My heart was beating so fast it was like I was riding a roller coaster! I sat in a window seat, and the takeoff was fun, but I did not like the air pockets we experienced on the flight. They felt like hitting potholes in a car. After a 2-hour flight, the plane landed safely, much to my relief. In those years, people could walk right up to the concourse gate and meet you, so when I exited the plane, my heart leaped when I saw my father and family there to meet me. I was so happy to see them, and they were glad to see me. Of course, they all joked at the New England accent I had acquired living with Mom, but by the time school started back in the fall, my accent was just as "country" as everyone else in our town.

Heartbreak

Just when things were looking up, another heartbreak hit my family. One afternoon, my younger siblings and I took a bike ride to a small store called *Hooper's*. Mr. Hooper ran the store, and he sold candy for a penny! My dad and stepmom were at work as usual. Like we had done many times before, we peddled by the church our family attended and took a left turn onto Church Street. In a single-file line, my stepsister, other sister, and I safely crossed. I glanced behind to check on my little brother's progress and watched in helpless horror as a car veered into my brother's path and slammed into him. It seemed like time slowed as I watched my brother get thrown into the air and crash back down onto the pavement.

I stared in shock, paralyzed, not believing what I had just seen. Instead of running to my brother, I ran into a nearby house with an open door and dialed "zero" for the operator. (911 didn't exist yet.) I told the operator our location and that we needed an ambulance immediately. When I returned to the scene, I found a circle of people gathered around my brother. Even though part of me desperately wanted to go to his side, I couldn't bring myself to get any closer. I felt like I was reliving the nightmare of losing my first brother, and I didn't want to see if he was alive or dead. I couldn't stand the thought of losing another brother!

The ambulance arrived, and paramedics began to work on my brother. By God's grace, my dad just happened to drive by the scene and stopped when he saw us. I can't even imagine what he felt or what went through his mind at that moment, especially after already losing one child. My brother was loaded into the ambulance and whisked off to the nearest hospital. I would later learn that the man who hit my brother was a drunk driver.

Though my father could've blamed God for what happened, I instead saw him draw closer to God during this trial, and his faith in dark times influenced me. Now, I look back at this moment and can see God at work on my family's behalf—though I couldn't see it at the time.

My brother was in bad condition. Doctors had to graft skin on some of his wounds and performed surgeries to insert rods and pins to help his broken bones heal. Our family prayed fervently for his recovery, but his hospital stay was long.

Prior to the accident, my stepmother worked fulltime as head teller at a Bi-Lo grocery store. Unwilling to leave my brother alone in the hospital, my stepmother took a leave of absence from work and drove 30 minutes daily to stay with him as he recovered.

All of a sudden, we became a one-income family, and the expenses of the hospital were overwhelming. My dad worked at a place called B&B Small Engines. He also had a small shop behind his house where he worked on small engines at home. During the day, he worked at his regular job. In the evening and into the night, he worked in his shop to try to keep up with the never-ending stream of bills. Everyone was stressed. The opportunity for a better life that I had dreamed of before coming to live with Dad was not turning out as I had hoped.

But despite the uncertainty of my brother's future and the overwhelming hours of work my father and stepmother were putting in, our family still went to church every Sunday morning and night. My dad and stepmother's income may have gone down, but they never lost their faith. In fact, it was that *faith* that I saw in them that drew me toward Christ.

My dad believed in tithing, and he frequently told us: "PAY YOUR TITHES." He did it faithfully, even when he had to make the difficult choice between paying his bills or his tithes. But my father trusted God and believed that if he was faithful in the test of paying his tithes, God would be faithful in blessing our family.

And God was very faithful to us. Even though Dad didn't go around asking for financial help, people from our community would randomly show up at our house with items to give us. People I didn't even know would come and say, "Tommy, (that's my dad's name) I have something for you," and they'd hand him money. On one particular instance, I remember a man from our church came over and gave my dad a $100. For us back then, that would've been like a $1,000! My father believed that God was sending these people to help us during our dark hour, and I started believing it, too. This God thing was new to me, but here I was watching God at work. The evidence was in front of my eyes that there was something more to God than just going to church. Little did I know at the time, a personal faith in God was taking root in me.

Jeans, Teeth, and Hair

When school was starting back up, we needed some new clothes. As parents know, kids outgrow their clothes fast! With our family finances strapped, Dad could only afford to buy each of us two pairs of pants and two shirts. My stepsister, who was my age, wore the same size pants and shirt as I did. Because Levi's jeans were the pants that most people wore at that time, my stepsister and I would rotate pants and shirts.

With my creative wardrobe solution in place, I began the 8th grade. This was the year I learned to take pride in myself. But first, I had to work through some things, beginning with my front teeth. One of my front teeth was chipped. When I was eight years old, my uncle was washing his car with a brush that had a long handle. I thought it would be funny to sneak up on him and surprise him, but he abruptly turned. The brush handle hit me right in the mouth, and *boom*, my tooth was chipped. Adding to my embarrassment, my other front tooth was longer than the chipped one. Kids being kids, my classmates made fun of my teeth, so I stopped smiling. I would even cover my mouth with my hand if I accidentally cracked a grin.

Finally, my stepmother decided we would do something about my tooth problems. She took me to the dentist. To my knowledge, it was the first time I had ever visited a dentist. And do you know what his solution to my dilemma was? He filed down the long tooth to match the length of the chipped one. And *presto*! I got my smile back!

When I returned to junior high, people noticed that my teeth were fixed, and I felt great. For the first time in my life, I was starting to feel good about myself. I was on the way up. What could possibly go wrong?

Well, my hair went wrong.

In the middle 70s and early 80s, it was popular for guys to part their hair in the middle and feather it back with *wings*. I would see all these guys with stylish hair in TV shows and commercials and try to copy their look. But my hair was not like most Caucasian hair. It was thicker, and when I tried to get it to part in the middle, it wouldn't lie flat. No matter what I tried, it would just naturally poof out in a literal *fro*, and being in junior high school, I became super self-conscious of it. So once again, my self-confidence plummeted.

My lack of confidence showed up in my school work. Even though I was one year older than most of my classmates since I had to repeat a grade, I was a terrible student. I was the picture of the kid who would be a nothing, who would do nothing good with their life. If you were to ask my teachers back then to predict my future, I'm sure they would've sighed that I'd turn into a high school dropout or a criminal or a drug addict.

My life was starting to look pretty hopeless. On top of all this, in the back of my mind, I was always terrified of dying—just like my little brother had.

$2 an Hour?!

Somehow, I made it through my 8th-grade year of junior high, and finally, something good came from being a year older than my class-mates: I got my learner's permit to drive a car. I started working with my father at his job. The business owner paid me a huge $2 an hour for after-school work and for an additional 2 1/2 hours of work on Saturday.

I loved working! It was at work that people finally started saying good things about me. They took notice of my hard work and praised me for it.

The business owner gave me a moped motorcycle to ride, and with my learner's permit, I could legally drive it on the road. Boy, did I think I was something riding on it all over town! It may have been my trans-portation, but it meant far more to me. To me, that moped was *freedom*.

Another summer came, and I got another job making $3 an hour sanding down cars at a body shop. Scrubbing down cars was hard work and not very pleasant in the summer heat, but I kept saving my money. And finally, the day came when I bought my first car, a 1976 Ford Pinto! I paid $775 for that car, and I was in love!

The car was yellow and had a black top, and whoever had owned it before me had installed metal covers that looked like a foot on the gas pedal and on the floor headlight dimmer switch. In hindsight, I was so excited about those cool features that I hardly noticed a poorly-done repair on the driver's side rear fender. The car had some other blemishes as well, but it was *A* car. It was *MY* car...even if I couldn't afford to pay the insurance on it at that time. So, I parked it at my dad's house and occasionally drove it around the yard.

Randy Brooks

That spring, the church my father and stepmother attended (and the one I was forced to attend), hired a youth pastor named Randy Brooks. This guy was not like anyone I had ever met. He was nice to me every time I met him. He invited me to a cookout at a church member's house, and I reluctantly accepted his invitation.

To my surprise, the cookout ended up being fun, and Randy even bragged on the way I played volleyball. Suddenly, I found myself liking this very friendly guy. When I would go to church, he always made sure to say "Hello, Jeff!"

When our church had its bus repainted at the body shop I worked at, guess who dropped in to check in on me. Yep, Randy. He even praised me in front of my coworkers, telling everyone what a hard worker I was. Up to this point in my life, I had never met someone who was so genuinely nice to me all the time. I believe that God used this man to begin tearing down self-protecting walls of hurt, anger, distrust, and fear that I had built in my early life.

Summer came again, and on one exceptionally hot July Sunday, our pastor ended the morning service, challenging everyone to return that night to see a movie about what life on earth would be like when Jesus returned for His church. Our church rarely showed movies during a service, so I was curious.

My family had lunch at my grandmother's house that day, and afterward, all my brothers, sisters, and cousins went outside to play a now-in-famous game called Yard Darts. The game consisted of placing plastic circles on the ground and throwing darts 20 feet into the air. The objective was to land as many darts in the circles as you could. Sounds harmless, BUT these were no ordinary darts. They were much larger than the dartboard variety. And being kids, we didn't just stand on the sidelines watching others throw their darts. To add even more risk to the game, two of us would stand in the circle and move out of the way just before the dart hit the ground. I remember dodging the incoming dart and laughing with my family about how it almost hit me. Yes, that was some of our family entertainment. A trip to the emergency room was always waiting in the wings!

And that's when my *opportunity for a better life* suddenly opened up in front of me.

When Life Changed

Though it may seem strange, right in the middle of all this excitement, noise, silliness, and danger, I felt something inside of me change. In my heart, I felt a yearning to know Jesus. I wanted Him in my life. I wanted to follow Him. As our family games continued, in my heart, I decided to become a Christ-follower. I made up my mind that when I got back to the church that night, I was going to walk down the aisle as soon as the pastor gave the invitation to come to the altar.

My family returned to the church that night. I sat in the back of the church with my stepsister and her friend. And then a hush fell over the audience as the movie started. I can't tell you much about the movie because the whole time, all I wanted was to go down to the altar to become a follower of Jesus. I grew impatient as the movie went on and on; I just wanted it to end! Finally, it finished, and sure enough, my pastor gave an invitation for those who wanted to commit their lives to Christ. Here was the moment—the opportunity I had been waiting for! But I hesitated. My eyes stared at the long aisle that led down to the altar. I felt antsy, queasy. Part of me wanted to run down the aisle; part of me wanted to remain seated, and part of me wanted to run out the door of the church.

But I felt an undeniable tug at my heart.

I finally got up, walked down the aisle, and knelt at the altar. I said to Jesus, "I don't know you. But if you can make me like Randy, I want to know you. Save me, Lord Jesus." That night I received an opportunity for a better life through Jesus Christ. From that day forward, my life has been on an upward climb to better and better things. That's not to say my life has been problem-free or stress-free since I chose to follow Jesus. On the contrary, life is always going to challenge us, many times in ways we can't foresee. But, as you will read about in the rest of this book, one of the amazing things about following Jesus is that you are no longer facing your life's challenges *alone*. And with God's help, your life can get better!

If you'd like to start a different path with your life, I will share with you some practical steps, that I have learned over more than 30 years of failure and success, that will help you begin a journey to a better life.

Are you ready to receive God's offer for an opportunity for a better life?

If you're ready, here's the starting point: Have you asked Jesus to be the Lord and Savior of your life? This is a very important question to answer because everything I will share with you in the rest of this book is founded on making that decision. This is where *your opportunity for a better life* starts.

Ready to start living a better life? If so, here is a simple prayer that you can say to express to God your desire to serve Him. If you mean it in your heart, you will be saved and become a follower of Jesus Christ.

Prayer to Become a Christ-follower

Dear Lord Jesus, I know I am a sinner, and I ask for Your forgiveness. I believe You died for my sins and rose from the dead. I will trust and follow You as my Lord and Savior. Guide my life and help me to do Your will.

In Jesus' name, Amen.

If you prayed that prayer or just read it and meant it, I want to welcome you to God's family! You just opened the door for God to do things in your life that you can't do for yourself. Your opportunity for a better life begins now.

If you are still not sure if you're ready to make this decision at this time, just mark this page and come back to it at any time.

Now that you have taken the first step or at least know the first step, congratulations! You have an *opportunity for a better life*.

Chapter 2

Keep Better Company

Have you ever been driving somewhere in a hurry, and suddenly the crossguards of a railroad crossing in front of you lower? As you stop and sit there, watching the train cars slowly pass by, it seems like the train is a hundred miles long. You start to wonder if the train will ever end! And then to your frustration, the train cars slow and eventually come to a complete stop, blocking your way. As you imagine this scene, watching the train pass, think about this: the train cars are all connected together and moving in the same direction. The only way to change the direction of one of those train cars is to disconnect it from the others.

I believe that our lives are like those train cars; we are connected together with the people in our lives. Said another way, the people in your life will determine the direction of your life more than anything else in the world. If you are not happy with the way your life is going, ask yourself these questions: "Who am I connected to? Who do I spend a lot of time around?"

Your connections will determine your direction.

It's been said that you are the average of the 5 people who are closest to you. Think about that. Who are the 5 people closest to you? Do you like the direction their lives are going? If not, maybe it's time to have an upgrade in your relationships so that your life can go in a new direction.

WHO Luck

I was listening to a John Maxwell leadership talk recently, and I heard him say something that made me think about the people I have met in my life. His statement was, "You need some *WHO LUCK* in your life." He went on to describe WHO LUCK as being who you meet and who you listen to and who you spend your time with. In ways you may not even see, these people are influencing your life and pulling you in their direction. Wow.

I'm going to make an even stronger statement now: I believe that your life is directly shaped by the people you connect yourself to and by the books you read. I have a strong personal belief in WHO LUCK. I've seen its amazing impact on my life, and I know beyond any doubt that my life would not be where it is today without the wonderful people I've connected with and the books I've read.

Speaking of books, let me take you to a story in my favorite one. In the Bible, the third chapter of Daniel records an example of the power of connecting with the right people, especially people strong in faith.

Just prior to the story, Nebuchadnezzar, king of Babylon, invaded Israel with his army, conquered the land, and took only the best Israelites as captives back to his capital city. Among the people captured were three young men, Shadrach, Meshach, and Abednego.

Nebuchadnezzar was a powerful king during that time and made his capital city, Babylon, one of the most beautiful in history. It even had "hanging gardens" so extraordinary that they became known as one of the seven wonders of the ancient world. Nebuchadnezzar had many structures and memorials built all over his kingdom to bring honor to his name, but one, in particular, outshined them all. He had a golden statue of himself, 90 feet high, constructed and then gave a royal decree that everyone in the kingdom *had* to bow down to it when music sounded each day. Nebuchadnezzar wanted to be worshiped like a god.

Now, before you start to say, "That guy is out of his mind," take a look around. We live in a world where we are constantly taught to collect status symbols. Our cars, our homes, jobs, boats, clothes, motorcycles, mobile phones, golf clubs, or even our children can become our "statues." I believe that most, if not all people, have a desire to be noticed. And if we're not careful and neglect to have godly connections in our lives, we could let this desire to be noticed take us places we never intended to go. Without realizing it, we could set ourselves up to do negative things we never thought we would do and bring much regret into our lives.

Fiery Trial

The story in the book of Daniel gets even more interesting. The three Hebrew men, Shadrach, Meshach, and Abednego, were faced with a huge dilemma. One of the Ten Commandments forbade them to worship idols. If they bowed to the statue—even though the king's law said they had to—they would be worshipping the king instead of God. But if they refused to bow, they would risk angering Nebuchadnezzar and possibly lose their lives.

I don't believe it was an easy decision for them. But being people of great character and faith, together they chose not to bow when the music was sounded.

So, picture this: A crowd of thousands gathers around a golden statue about as tall as a 9-story building with blinding sunlight bouncing off its towering form. A tremendous noise of instruments strikes up and blares through the air. Immediately, all of the people fall to the ground in worship of Nebuchadnezzar's image—all, except for the three Hebrew men.

Do you think anyone noticed? Absolutely! With everyone flat to the ground, Shadrach, Meshach, and Abednego stood out like three brave statues themselves. Know that when you choose to take a stand for godly principles, people will take notice no matter how big the crowd is. Some will applaud your courage, and others will do everything in their power to undermine you.

People in the crowd already hated them because they were for-eigners and because they worshiped a different God. They also didn't like that these three had earned prestigious jobs in the king's own gov-ernment. Whether from prejudice or jealousy or anger or a desire to take their place, the enemies of Shadrach, Meshach, and Abednego went before the king and appealed to him. Here's what happened in Daniel 3:12-15 (NIV):

> But there are some Jews whom you have set over the affairs of the province of Babylon—Shadrach, Meshach and Abednego—who pay no attention to you, Your Majesty. They neither serve your gods nor worship the image of gold you have set up." Furious with rage, Nebuchadnezzar summoned Shadrach, Meshach and Abednego. So these men were brought before the

king and Nebuchadnezzar said to them, "Is it true, Shadrach, Meshach and Abednego, you do not serve my gods or worship the image of gold I have set up? Now when you hear the sound of the horn, flute, zither, lyre, harp, pipe and all kinds of music, if you are ready to fall down and worship the image I made, very good. But if you do not worship it, you will be thrown immediately into a blazing furnace. Then what god will be able to rescue you from my hand?" So the king was giving them a second chance to rethink their decision to bow or not to bow.

In his book *All In*, Mark Batterson points out that it was Shadrach, Meshach, and Abednego's *integrity* that got them into trouble with the king. They held strong to their beliefs and refused to bow down to the idol. They refused to bend their beliefs to whatever crowd they were around and remained true to their standards no matter who they were with. This characteristic of a person's life is *integrity*.

You might say, "Why bother having integrity when it can get you thrown into a fiery furnace?" My answer is that there is a very powerful flipside to this dilemma, and it's one that can be a gamechanger in your life. Here's the remarkable principle in three words: Integrity pleases God.

Think about it: What could you do if God were on your side? Sit with that question for a moment before continuing.

The WE Factor

Look at how the three Hebrew men responded to the king's ultimatum in Daniel 3:16-18 (NIV):

Shadrach, Meshach and Abednego replied to him, "King Nebuchadnezzar, we do not need to defend ourselves before you in this matter. If we are thrown into the blazing furnace, the God we serve is able to deliver us from it, and he will deliver us from Your Majesty's hand. But even if he does not, we want you to know, Your Majesty, that we will not serve your gods or worship the image of gold you have set up.

When I read their bold and courageous reply, my adrenaline starts pumping like I'm watching an old *Rocky* movie. The underdog has spoken, and I'm pulling for them. I find myself saying, *"You go, Shadrach, Meshach, and Abednego!"*

But if you and I are not careful, we'll miss one of the most powerful points about this story. I call it the WE FACTOR. Look back at their response and notice how many times they said *we*. The WE FACTOR is this: *WE* is always stronger than *ME*. The three Hebrew men made a decision to stand together for their values, principles, and faith in God. Had two of them chosen to bow down, the others may have folded under pressure. I believe they had to remind each other of what they were going to do and why they were going to do it.

When you don't have the WE FACTOR at work in your life, situations can become overwhelming to the point that you will want to bow down. Shadrach, Meshach, and Abednego had a common connection to God and to each other, which strengthened their resolve, their integrity, and energized them to look death in the eye and say, "Know this King: If we die, you are not taking our lives from us; we are giving them to God."

Solomon, called the wisest man who ever lived, described the power of the WE FACTOR this way in Ecclesiastes 4:9-10, 12 (NIV):

Two are better than one, because they have a good return for their labor: If either of them falls down, one can help the other up. But pity anyone who falls and has no one to help them up... Though one may be overpowered, two can defend themselves. A cord of three strands is not quickly broken.

Just because the three Hebrew men stood up for what was right didn't mean that suddenly everything went great for them. On the contrary, the greatest test of their integrity, beliefs, and faith was about to begin. But it is also in this deadly test of faith that we can see the spiritual implication of the WE FACTOR. Look at Daniel 3:19-25:

Then Nebuchadnezzar was furious with Shadrach, Meshach and Abednego, and his attitude toward them changed. He ordered the furnace heated seven times hotter than usual and commanded some of the strongest soldiers in his army to tie up Shadrach, Meshach and Abednego and throw them into the blazing furnace. So these men, wearing their robes, trousers, turbans and other clothes, were bound and thrown into the blazing furnace. The king's command was so urgent and the furnace so hot that the flames of the fire killed the soldiers who took up Shadrach, Meshach and Abednego, and these three men, firmly tied, fell into the blazing furnace. Then King Nebuchadnezzar leaped to his feet in amazement and asked his advisers, "Weren't there three men that we tied up and threw into the fire?" They replied, "Certainly, Your Majesty." He said, "Look! I see four men walking around in the fire, unbound and unharmed, and the fourth looks like a son of the gods." (NIV)

The spiritual implication of the WE FACTOR is that when we connect together as believers, God shows up in supernatural ways. Jesus said it this way in Matthew 18:20 (NIV):

For where two or three gather in my name, there am I with them.

We is always stronger than *me* because God shows up in our lives and can do what we can't even imagine! I don't want to sound like a prophet of doom, but in life, difficult times come our way, sometimes when we least expect it. You may be going through something right now that is absolutely overwhelming you. I want to encourage you to make the decision right now to surround yourself with people of faith to harness the WE FACTOR in your life. Don't try to carry your burden alone.

Hope or Toast?

So what happened to Shadrach, Meshach, and Abednego? Daniel 3:26-28 (NIV) records the astonishing end to their story:

Nebuchadnezzar then approached the opening of the blazing furnace and shouted, "Shadrach, Meshach and Abednego, servants of the Most High God, come out! Come here!" So Shadrach, Meshach and Abednego came out of the fire, and the satraps, prefects, governors and royal advisers crowded around them. They saw that the fire had not harmed their bodies, nor was a hair of their heads singed; their robes were not scorched, and there was no smell of fire on them. Then Nebuchadnezzar said, "Praise be to the God of Shadrach, Meshach and Abednego, who has sent his angel and rescued his servants! They trusted in him and defied the king's command and were willing to give up their lives rather than serve or worship any god except their own God.

It's important to understand that the WE FACTOR may not keep you out of the fire, but it can keep you from getting burned while you are going through the fire. Interestingly, the only things burned by the fire were the things that bound them up! When a fiery trial threatens to scorch your life, don't go alone. And know that as you go through the fire, God may be at work, unseen in the background, freeing you from something that has been binding you up for a long time.

I have come to this conclusion about life:

You don't know nothing until you've been through something.

While you are going through *the something*, you need someone you can lean on in order to stay focused on God while you are in the process of being set free.

I believe we all need people in our lives who are going in the same direction we want to go. If you take a look at the people who you are frequently around, and they are people who are just "getting by," you may want to "upgrade" your friends. Think about this question: WHO is going to be the WHO in your life that helps you go in a new direction?

In the church I pastor, we set up a way for this to happen through our small group program. Groups of people meet once a week to talk about the Bible and life. In my life, church has been one of my greatest sources of God's blessings through WHO LUCK.

And this WHO LUCK didn't just start when I became a pastor. In my life, it began all the way back when I was a teenager, and I first asked Jesus into my heart during a Sunday evening service at church. Afterward, I prayed two additional prayers that day. One prayer was, "Lord, help me be like Randy Brooks" (my youth pastor at the time). I prayed the other prayer when I got home: "Jesus, give me a girlfriend who can help me stay sexually pure." God was listening and answered my prayers.

Life-changing Trip

After I asked Jesus to save me and went public with my decision by being baptized, Randy told me how proud he was of my decision to receive Jesus into my life. He invited me on a youth trip to a place called Deep Creek in Bryson City, North Carolina. Deep Creek was just that—a creek deep enough that people could float on innertubes. I loved the outdoors! So add in camping, tubing down a creek, friends, and *girls*, and I thought this was going to be one of the best trips ever!

Interestingly, this camping trip became the beginning of the answer to my prayer for a godly girlfriend. As our group launched out onto the river on our innertubes, two teenage girls caught my eye. One girl, named Kelly, had an outgoing, energetic personality. The other girl was quiet but, yet, somehow adventurous. Her name was Rhonda. Thanks to the awkwardness I felt about my appearance, I wasn't that self-confident, and both of these girls were pretty. I wondered, "How can I impress them?" I thought back to my family, and one thing that my family loved to do was laugh and make people laugh. So, as we floated down the creek, I maneuvered my innertube close to them and started saying things to try to get them to laugh. And guess what—they did!

Floating down the river, I found that my heart leaped when I was around the quiet girl. She liked to laugh, and I liked making her laugh. I started wondering if maybe this girl would want to date me.

To Date or Not to Date

The rest of the trip was great. I got to know everyone in the group much better, but my mind kept going back to Rhonda. I decided that when I got back home, I was going to court her. But, when I got back home, the dreaded fear of rejection set in. Mentally, I went back and forth whether to call her or not. I'd get the guts up and then back down. My stomach was all knotted with my emotions.

Finally, I decided that my desire to be Rhonda's boyfriend was worth the risk and more important than being rejected. So I hurried to the phone in our house and picked up our small town's phone book. With my heart starting to race a little, I turned to the page where her family's last name would fall and ran my finger down the columns of names. And then, there it was—her last name with the number listed beside it! I nearly passed out!

I collected myself, took a deep breath, and picked up the phone's receiver. Since this was the 1980s, the telephone was physically attached to the wall and connected to the handset by a long cord. Because we had a rotary dial phone, I put my finger in the hole over the first number and turned it to the left in a circular motion. I released the dialer and waited for it to spin back to its starting place. Phone numbers were only five digits back then, so after shakily putting in four more numbers, I waited. I worried, "What if she doesn't want to talk to me."

Suddenly, there was a click, and a voice answered on the other line. My heart was really pumping now!

But it wasn't Rhonda. Her sister politely asked who was calling. I don't know if my voice squeaked, but I nervously asked if I could speak with Rhonda. I heard, "Hold on," followed by her name being called in the background. Ug, more waiting! But now I couldn't think of what I should say. Uh oh, I hadn't thought that far ahead. I thought about saying, "Hey Rhonda, you're so fine, you've gotta be mine!" Or maybe, "Rhonda, I know your feet have to be tired...because you've been runnin' through my mind all day!"

And then she answered!

When I heard her sweet voice on the phone, my heart skipped! I was so overwhelmed, my mind blanked, and to this day, I can't even remember what I said to her next! What I can tell you is that something beautiful between us started that day and continues on more than 30 years later!

As Rhonda and I began to date, I didn't realize it at the time, but behind the scenes, God was sending more mentors into my life. Whereas my family was loud and boisterous, her family was reserved and quiet. Her father, mother, and sister were all extremely friendly and thoughtful—qualities I was not used to. In my family, there were so many of us that it felt like it was every person for themselves. I learned that Rhonda's dad didn't have to use the power of grounding or spanking when she was growing up. He used the power of respect. And in turn, Rhonda didn't want to disappoint him in any way. Her mother is the greatest example of someone filled with a desire to serve and help people that I have ever witnessed. To this day, whenever we visit, Rhonda's mom always welcomes us with open arms and says, "Let me fix you something to eat."

From the first day I met them, they treated me like I was their own son, and I can't even put into words how much that means to me. My father was a man who worked hard, but when he came home each day, he expected to be able to sit in his recliner and relax. My stepmother has a serving heart, so she was more than happy to serve my father food and drink while he chilled in his recliner. If his glass of tea was empty, all he had to do was shake the ice cubes in the glass, and my stepmother would whisk the glass away, refill it with tea, and return it to my dad's hand. As I grew up watching this, I missed the point that my stepmother was choosing to serve my father in this way, and as a teenager, I boldly thought, "When I get married, that's how my wife is going to treat me."

Tying the Knot

When Rhonda and I married, I was expecting our life together to be a blissful paradise. Don't get me wrong; I understood that problems would come up—they always do in life—but I expected her to serve me just like I had seen my stepmother serve my dad. I really had no idea how much my one-sided concepts of a husband and wife relationship were about to get shaken like an earthquake!

Being newlyweds just starting out, we didn't have much furniture. Most of what we owned had been given to us by other people. But when we could afford to buy a new piece of furniture, take a guess at what we bought. (Think back to the story about my father I just shared.) If you guessed a *recliner*, you're right!

As the new chair was being delivered, I was already having visions of me sitting in it after a long day of work and of Rhonda serving me fresh sweet tea every time that I jingled the ice in my empty glass.

And then, the moment came! I was kicked back in my new recliner, a grin on my face, an almost-empty glass of tea in my hand. I finished off the bit left with a swig and shook the glass so that the ice cubes inside it rattled around. And I waited...and waited. I threw a glance over at Rhonda. To my surprise, she seemed to be ignoring me! Didn't she know the code? Didn't she know that when I rattled my empty glass it meant that she needed to stop whatever it was she was doing and immediately whisk away my cup to the kitchen, refill it, and bring it back to me?

I was confused. In my father's house, he never had to shake his empty glass twice. My stepmother always promptly refilled his cup. "What's going on here?" I wondered. "Maybe Rhonda didn't hear me," I convinced myself.

So, I shook the glass even harder and louder.

After a moment, Rhonda looked over at me with a puzzled expression and asked, "Is there something wrong with your hand?"

This was the beginning of two very different people from two very different backgrounds learning to become one. Soon, we discovered other differences between our raisings. Rhonda's dad helped with the housework; my dad did not do housework. Her dad was a friendly man who didn't want to trouble anyone. My father was a take-charge person who showed love and respect in a different way. In hindsight, I'm very grateful that I got to know both ways of being a father. Knowing both have helped make me into a more rounded, caring, and strong leader in my family.

If you want an opportunity for a better life, you must surround yourself with good people.

Buses and Bicycles

Another person during this time who played a key role in my personal development was my youth pastor, Randy Brooks. After I made my decision to follow Jesus, I wanted to be around Randy. He always made me feel special, and he showed me how to live the life of a Christian.

When Rhonda and I dated, we'd hang out at Randy and his wife Sheila's house on a Friday night or at a church youth event there. I would do anything I could to hang out with him. He taught me why reading the Bible was so important for a Christian. He taught me how to pray and handle many of life's challenges. However, the most important things he taught me were to love and serve God. He believed these two things could give a person the greatest fulfillment in life.

So, as an excited and highly-motivated teenager, I began to serve in church by literally trying my hand at everything. First, I volunteered to help with our church's bus ministry. I met Randy and other team members every Saturday, and we would go door-to-door, knocking and asking people to come to our church. If the parents didn't want to go, we offered to come by and pick up their children with our bus on Sunday morning.

Then on Sunday mornings, I would meet the bus driver and ride along as we traveled our bus route to the homes of the families who had agreed to attend. I enjoyed seeing the kids we picked up every Sunday, but my favorite part of the ride was being with Randy. He always encouraged me by saying things like, "Jeff, you did a great job!" and, "Jeff, you're a special person!"

After Randy mentored me for a little while, he asked me to be a bus captain, which meant I would be responsible for making the Saturday, cold-call visits and for telling the driver which houses to stop at on

Sunday morning. It was my first leadership job, and I was stoked! But there was just one problem: I wasn't old enough to drive yet! So, if no one was available to drive me on my Saturday route, I had to ride my bicycle to make my visits.

On one memorable Saturday, when I had to ride my bike across town, I rode into a rundown trailer park where one of my bus kids lived. I walked up to a weather-beaten door and knocked. With a squeak, the door opened, and a man, covered in tattoos and who I didn't recognize, stared curiously at me. I announced that I was there to see if the child living there wanted to go to church the next day. With a slight grunt, he invited me inside the trailer. As I entered the living room and took in my surroundings, I noticed white powder on a table and a stack of money beside it. I learned later that this man had just gotten out of jail.

You'd think I'd be scared in that moment, but I felt courage come over me.

The man spoke up, asking me about my faith. He was particularly interested in why I would ride my bicycle miles to invite people to church. I remember searching through my mind, thinking, "What would Randy say to this man if he were here?" I responded with the only thought that came: "Because Jesus saved me, and I believe He wants to save everyone." I will never forget the look on that man's face as I said that. His menacing appearance melted, and he looked like he was about to cry. With a sincere nod, he said that I was doing something good.

I left the trailer unharmed and with a profound sense that God had been with me the whole time. I don't remember seeing that man at our church. The child who lived there didn't ride my bus to church for very long. His family moved shortly after my visit. But I'm still thankful for at least being able to introduce them to the idea of going to church.

Youth Sunday

Randy challenged me to do things that I thought I couldn't do. One day, he had an idea for our small church to have a "Youth Sunday." The concept was to have the teenagers of the church do everything in the church on that Sunday morning. So, Randy asked me to teach the Senior Men's Bible Class. Talk about intimidating!

I was only 16, and I had a great fear of reading in front of other people. Our Sunday School curriculum used a large lesson plan book that the teacher read from, while standing in front of the class. After imagining myself having to read lengthy passages in front of a group of senior men, I immediately went back to Randy and told him that I didn't think I could do it. In his usual calm, encouraging way, he smiled at me and replied that he felt I could do it and that I needed to give it a try. I groaned inside myself, very worried about what I was going to sound like reading in front of those people, but I agreed to teach the class that Sunday.

And guess what! Youth Sunday came, and when it was time to start class, I took my place at the lectern in front of the room. I hesitantly looked out across the rows of chairs, and all I saw were a bunch of eyes staring back at me. I felt my stomach lurch within me. I took a deep breath, swallowed hard, and began the class. I'm sure my voice was shaky as I started speaking, and I know that I stumbled on all kinds of words as I tried to read through pages of information from the teacher's book. A part of me just wanted the whole experience to be over as quickly as possible!

My first teaching experience wasn't pretty, and, in truth, it was probably a train wreck. But, after the class was over, many of the senior men came up to me and told me that I had done a great job. In hindsight, I know that they were trying to encourage me, and I think they were just excited to see someone young taking an interest in teaching the Bible. Plus, having gone through decades of life themselves, they knew that if a person continues to practice at something, they'll get better. But at that moment, if you would've told me that God would end up using me to teach countless people about His principles for living, I think I would've laughed hysterically at you.

And yet, despite my shortcomings, God had a great plan for my life. So take heart! I believe that despite your shortcomings, God has a plan for you, too.

First Sermon

With the success of Youth Sunday, Randy then had a grand idea to put on a youth revival. The services would start on a Sunday and continue nightly through Wednesday. I wondered who the Sunday night speaker would be. Then, to my shock and dread, Randy asked *me* to be the Sunday night speaker! I was honored that he'd ask me—but quite a bit surprised since my 17-year old self still lacked a lot of confidence.

After mulling over the request, I decided that speaking at the revival was not for me. I felt I wasn't ready to take such a big leap. So, I went to Randy and told him I couldn't do it. He gave me one of his classic facial expressions and replied, "If anyone can do this, *you can*. I believe in you, Jeff."

Reluctantly, I agreed to speak at the revival.

To say that I was scared would be the understatement of the year! Up to this point, I had now taught a few Sunday School classes, served in the nursery, and given a few testimonies from the stage. But to deliver an entire sermon in front of the whole church? "Not me!" would have been my reaction. However, in my prayer time with God, I had been asking Him if He wanted me to be a preacher. As a sign of confirmation, I told God that if He wanted me to preach, He'd have to get someone to ask me to speak. Only God and I knew about this agreement, and then suddenly, here was Randy asking me to speak.

But even though I believed I had been given a direct confirmation from God, I still felt terribly underprepared and out of my league! I knew I needed help, so I turned once again to God. I prayed, "Okay, Lord...I hear You. I can't believe you work so fast! I need Your help!" Once again, my fear of reading in front of people was haunting me. I knew that if I became a preacher, I would have to read out loud a LOT, and this idea scared me more than anything else.

Having to face my fear publicly terrified me! Through my early life, I had learned how to cover up my reading difficulties. But I knew that if I preached, my hidden insecurity would be exposed like a spotlight on a prisoner trying to escape from jail.

And then my fears turned to images of failure. I agonized, "What if I flop? Will people make fun of me like they did in school?" Fear was squeezing my heart tightly.

Let me tell you: When God gives you an opportunity to do something great, you will face fear. Each of us will face different types of fear, but I encourage you to look at the fear as a sign that you have been given a great opportunity and that a personal breakthrough is just on the other side of that fear!

Having agreed to speak, Randy gave me the Bible verse John 12:32 to speak on. Here's what the verse says:

"And I, if I be lifted up from the earth, will draw all men unto me." (KJV)

After I read the verse, panic seized my mind. I had NO idea what to do with this verse or even how to come up with what to say in a sermon! At least in Sunday School, we had a curriculum that told the teacher exactly what to say. Now I was in completely uncharted waters. What would I say? How could I turn one short verse into an entire message? Time was ticking by quickly.

I shared with Randy an urgent plea for help. He gave me a few tips and then strongly suggested I meet with our pastor, Dan Hampton, to get better sermon preparation pointers. After a short conversation, the pastor agreed to meet with me after a Sunday night service to share with me how he created his sermons. I breathed a sigh of relief! I knew that he was a great preacher, so I believed that he'd teach me the "magic formula" to construct a powerful message.

After the Sunday night service, Pastor Hampton escorted me to his office. I eyed the bookcases filled with Bible commentaries and other study resources along the wall and wondered if I'd need to use them. Pastor Hampton sat down at his desk, and I pulled up a chair to the side. For the next 15 minutes, he gave me a mini-lesson on how to write a sermon. His lesson seemed rather short, and I kept wondering, "Surely there has to be more to this." His tips were good, but I was still in the dark as to how I was going to speak for an hour on just one Bible verse. Like everyone else who I'd spoken with about my dilemma, my pastor assured me that if I prayed, God would be with me when I spoke and that He would give me the words to speak at that moment.

I left his office with mixed emotions. Part of me felt excited because people believed in me and felt that I could do this. But part of me felt dread because I didn't know *how* I was going to do this.

I went home and began working on my Sunday message. I put my pastor's sermon-writing advice into action and continued working on my message off and on until the deadline arrived. But when the night of the revival finally came, I glanced over my message notes, and a twinge of worry filled me. My sermon looked very short! Uh oh.

Back during this time, guest speakers would sit up on the stage with the pastor in what we called the "holy men" chairs. I was nervous enough as it was, but on top of that, I had to endure the crowd's stares long before I spoke. And talk about a crowd! The place was packed! As the choir sang a song, which seemed to fly by, I remember thinking, "I wish some of these people had stayed home!"

And then a hush fell over the room, and Randy walked to the pulpit and introduced me.

My heart was in my throat! I briefly thought of darting off stage and letting Randy or the pastor deliver the message—but, of course, I couldn't do that. I stood up, a bit wobbly, and made what seemed like a mile-long walk to the pulpit at the front center of the stage.

I plunked my Bible down onto the big wooden pulpit and shuffled through my few pages of notes, arranging them in the right order. I cleared my throat and looked out over the crowd. My eyes naturally settled upon the back right of the sanctuary where my dad had been sitting for years. Yep, he was there, watching me. No pressure.

Everyone stared at me, waiting for me to begin.

I steadied myself by holding the pulpit, cleared my throat again, and launched into my message. I confess it all became a blur. I don't remember a lot of what I said. To my embarrassment, I do remember saying the word "sex" (in its proper context) in my message—but I didn't know that saying *that* word was taboo in our church! I glanced over at the back corner just in time to see my dad's head roll back as if he were saying, "Noooooooo!" But it was too late; I had already said it.

A speedy 10 minutes later, I finished my first sermon.

I was surprised by the reactions of the audience. They showed me great appreciation. I even had many people tell me afterward that I had done a good job. I thank God for those people because I knew that I hadn't done a fantastic job, but their encouragement convinced me that maybe I could actually preach and teach.

Afterward, Randy told me something that went straight to my heart and that I reflected back on many times when I felt discouraged. He said, "Jeff, I think you can become a preacher." I believe that God was using Randy in my life to help me become better. He was helping build my self-confidence. He saw something good in me that I couldn't see about myself. And then, he'd raise the bar of expectation on my life to stretch me and to help me grow.

If you want to be better, you must surround yourself with better people.

Randy made me better by believing in me and giving me opportunities to develop my self-confidence and talents. We served together for 3 years at the church, and then he accepted a position at another church. I was sad when he moved away. Nevertheless, he continued to mentor me over the phone, even challenging me to become a licensed minister and to seek out ministerial training. In truth, I didn't want to do either, but because he had such a strong faith in me and my potential, I made the decision to do *both*.

A Big Break!

After graduating from high school, Rhonda and I married. That may seem very young by today's norms, but it was quite normal back then.

Today, it's also assumed that after high school, a student will continue on to college. Because my parents didn't graduate from high school, I never even thought about going to college. To me, at the time, my high school diploma was an outstanding academic achievement for my family to celebrate!

After Rhonda and I married, we both worked decent jobs and made a good living. But...all the time, in the back of my head, I had a nagging feeling that I needed to do something else with my life—that I needed to be a youth pastor, like Randy.

A restlessness within stirred me to do something different—something of purpose, something of eternal value. So, as soon as I heard of a church that was looking for a student pastor, I would call them! And even though I was only 20, I ended up interviewing for youth-pastor job openings all over. I didn't get the jobs, but I kept trying.

Once again, Randy moved; this time to work with his father-in-law north of Atlanta. This city was a whole new world compared to the small town I had lived in most of my life. When Rhonda and I visited, we felt like fish out of water! But Randy and his wife Sheila were extremely kind, and we were just happy to see them.

And then something exciting happened! My big break into ministry was finally about to happen!

After Randy had been at his current church a few years, he learned that he was going to be promoted to an associate pastor. When he moved into the position, their church was going to need a student pastor, so who do you think he called and offered the position to? Yep! Rhonda and me.

I was excited! I was on cloud nine! I just knew that it was God's will for us to take this big leap of faith into youth ministry!

Rhonda, on the other hand...

Well, I'm not so sure that she felt the same way that I did. If we moved, we would have to leave behind everything that we had known up to that point in our lives, and that's a big sacrifice. We'd have to get new jobs in a town that we knew nothing about and have to start all over making new friends and getting to know a whole church full of people. Even closer to our hearts, we'd no longer be able to see our families as often—and Rhonda is extremely close to her family. I'm sure the decision was hard for her. But let me tell you something: God truly blessed me with an amazing wife! Regardless of the sacrifice, she loves God, and she loves me, and at that moment, she was willing to do whatever I thought God wanted us to do.

So, we packed up our belongings, said goodbye to our family, friends, and church, and moved to the city. It was our first big step of faith. And we didn't wait around to get busy.

Rhonda and I found jobs to provide income, and we started getting to know the people at Randy's church. We were settling in, and the people liked us. I just knew this was going to be an incredible opportunity to minister to the youth of this church.

And then a phone call came.

On the other end of the line was Dan Hampton, the former pastor of my home church. He was holding a revival at a church in Toccoa—a small town located in the northeast corner of Georgia. The pastor of the Toccoa church, Jerry Chitwood, had shared with my former pastor that there would be an opening for a student pastor soon. He invited me to tag along with him to one of the revival services to meet Reverend Chitwood.

After hanging up the phone, I was torn inside. I really didn't want to move again so soon. Rhonda and I had just finished unpacking the last of our moving boxes, and we liked the people of our new church. At the same time, I wondered if God was opening a ministry door for us. Despite my feelings, I wanted to be obedient to God—*if* this was God's leading. I had to find out.

So, I drove to Toccoa for the revival. There, I met Pastor Chitwood. He was a very cheerful, lively person with a booming voice, and he requested that Rhonda and I return for a formal interview. When I got home, and after I shared everything with Rhonda, she was silent. She gave me "the look"—which I have come to understand means that she is weighing out the possibilities and impacts of what I've just said. Like me, she had misgivings about leaving the work we had just started. Neither of us wanted to repack all of our belongings, resign from our new jobs, and try to find housing in yet another new area. But like me, Rhonda loves God and wants to honor Him with her life. After some more deliberating, we drove to Toccoa for our interview.

The interview went very well, so well that Pastor Chitwood felt that God wanted us to become the youth pastors at his church! I remember feeling a strong confirmation inside that this was where we needed to be. So once again, Rhonda and I packed up our stuff and moved to a new church.

And God was definitely guiding us. The people in the Toccoa church welcomed us warmly, and we made many friendships there. Rhonda and I also preferred the small-town feel. And most importantly, the two of us grew spiritually as we ministered to the youth of the church and area—one of them being a young girl named Chesnee, who would end up playing a pivotal role in my future ministry.

Through Pastor Chitwood's mentoring, I learned a great deal about leadership and ministry. Our 3 years of service with him seemed to fly by...But changes were coming.

More Changes

A position in our denomination's state headquarters opened, and Pastor Chitwood moved into this new role. With him no longer at the Toccoa church, I felt a new restlessness. Pastoral changes are usually very hard on a youth/associate pastor. Many times, the new pastor has a very different personality and way of doing things than the previous pastor. Some associate pastors adjust to the new reality without much difficulty, but many seek out positions at another church—which can be a good thing for the new pastor and the youth/associate pastor. After I learned that my former pastor, Dan Hampton, was hiring a youth pastor for his church, I felt I needed to make another move.

So once again, Rhonda and I loaded up our belongings, said our goodbyes, and moved, this time to Stone Mountain, Georgia. Stone Mountain was very different from Toccoa. The area was far more developed and did not have a small-town feel. But I was thrilled to be able to work with Pastor Hampton. He was a very tall man, who was so filled with energy that he hated to just stand still. He always had to be doing something, even if it was just whistling a tune as he walked down the hall. I also called him the "Singing Preacher" because he had to sing a song before he started preaching.

Working for Pastor Hampton, I learned how to step into a bolder role as more of an associate pastor (even though I was the youth pastor). He liked me and encouraged me to step out on faith, especially in regards to ministry.

And I did. The area was culturally diverse, so I started reaching out to the teens of the community to get them to come to our youth service. Taking a page from my early years of bus ministry, I would pick them up and bring them to youth service. We even purchased an old bus to do just that—but this time, I drove the bus instead of riding along as a bus monitor.

The number of teens attending our Wednesday-night youth service grew. I found out that one of the teens in the group, named Joey Oliver, could play piano, so I got him to play music for our youth worship time. I could feel the momentum of growth building, and I started feeling like I was going to be at this church for a long time.

And then I got sucker-punched!

This particular day started off like normal, but then Pastor Hampton invited me into his office for a private conversation. I started thinking, "Uh, oh. Have I done something wrong?" I felt like I was in the principal's office.

With a grin, he told me that I wasn't in trouble but that he wanted me to be one of the first people to know that he had accepted a promotion in our denomination's leadership and that he'd be leaving soon.

My stomach turned. I was speechless. Our church had *just started* a building program! The possibility of him moving hadn't even crossed my mind.

I thought, "Oh boy, here we go again." I started wondering how I would handle the transition of leadership to a new pastor. What would the new pastor be like? Would we get along? Would he like me as a person? Would I have to seek out a youth pastor job elsewhere?

After the meeting, I got alone with God and told Him exactly how I felt about the whole situation. And I confessed to Him that I didn't know if I could continue being a youth pastor if that meant that I was going to have to move every time there was a pastoral change at the church.

And then a new, radical thought occurred to me: *Should I become a pastor?*

In my prayer, I told God that I would become a pastor if it was what He wanted me to do. But I also made one big request of Him. I didn't want to move around like so many pastors in our denomination do; I wanted to pastor one congregation for the rest of my ministerial life.

I came away from my prayer time with faith that God was going to work something out—I just didn't know how or when.

And at first, there was no direct answer. The new pastor came in, and I worked hard for him. I tried my best to understand his way of doing things, but the two of us just didn't get along. He didn't seem very happy with me, and I wasn't very happy working for him. My prayer life became very strong during this period, but I started wondering if I'd misunderstood what I needed to do.

Then, I received a call from Pastor Chitwood, who now worked in our denomination's state office. He didn't want to get my hopes up too much but told me about an opportunity to pastor a small church in Forest Park, Georgia. Something inside of me connected with what he was saying on the phone, and I told him to count me in!

It's truly amazing for me to think back on all of these twists and turns my life took to get me to where I am now, but that opportunity to become the pastor of that small Forest Park church was God's answer to my prayer! And just like I requested, over 20 years later, I'm still pastoring the same congregation. The church has moved and merged and gone through name changes, but SCC continues to grow beyond what I could've even imagined in those earlier days of ministry!

The WHO FACTOR is one of the greatest tools God uses to develop us throughout our life. You can't choose your physical family, but you can choose your friends and your spiritual family. I encourage you to find a church that you can connect with people WHO can help guide you into a better life.

Chapter 3

The Power of the Sabbath

This may sound strange, but for me, work is like an addiction. I'm a "Type A" personality, internally driven to constantly be doing something and to accomplish as much as I possibly can every hour of every day of every week of every month of every year! Hello, my name is Jeff; I'm a workaholic.

So whenever I came across Bible verses that talked about rest or the *Sabbath*, I just kind of glazed over them. I knew they were there; I knew they were important. I even preached on them. My problem was that I just didn't think they applied to *me*. "I was doing God's work!" I thought. "No time to rest! Gotta win one more to Jesus! I can rest when I'm in heaven!"

As I've grown wiser with age, I can see that pulling 80-hour work weeks without some special time to rest is harmful to our lives. We may be able to endure it for a while, but this type of living eventually catches up with us—trust me, I know firsthand.

Without rest, our bodies are not able to effectively repair themselves. And just like if you own a car and keep putting off getting its oil changed, month after month after month, it will eventually break down, usually when you least need it to.

To live a fulfilling and effective life, I believe that we should take regularly scheduled time for rest. But you don't have to take my word for it. Take a look at Exodus 20:8-11:

> Remember the Sabbath day by keeping it holy. Six days you shall labor and do all your work, but the seventh day is a Sabbath to the LORD your God. On it you shall not do any work, neither you, nor your son or daughter, nor your male servant or female servant, nor your animals, nor any foreigner residing in your towns. For in six days the LORD made the heavens and the earth, the sea, and all that is in them, but he rested on the seventh day. Therefore the LORD blessed the Sabbath day and made it holy. (NIV)

Apparently, God felt that it was so important that we take regular time to rest that He made it the 4th Commandment! Think about that. God designed our bodies, and the Creator knows exactly what we need. He felt so strongly about us taking time to rest that He didn't just make it a suggestion; He made it a *commandment*. And I'd been skipping out on it for years.

And here's the funny part: I thought that because I was coming to church on Sunday and teaching God's principles for life to a room full of people in three or four services that I was observing the Sabbath. Ouch!

So how have I changed my actions and thinking in relation to rest and the Sabbath? Well, I wish I could say that I'm no longing driven to have to do something every minute of the day. Part of me still is, and I still struggle with this. What I'm learning to do is to *give myself permission to rest*.

You may ask, "Why do you have to give yourself permission to rest? That sounds silly." For me and for many of you reading this book, it is not a laughing matter. Let me share with you *why*.

Shocking Revelation

In 2007, I joined a coaching network for pastors that met in Tampa, Florida. The leader of the network is a pastor himself, so he knows all about what pulpit ministry is like from the inside.

In one session, which I will remember for the rest of my life, he started talking about the importance of honoring the Sabbath. Probably like most of the pastors in the room, I yawned within myself because I felt like this was something that I was already doing a great job at.

Casually, the speaker asked us which one of the Ten Commandments was okay to break or ignore. A rustling filled the room as all these pastors suddenly started paying attention. A few murmured to their neighbor, "*What did he just say?*"

Our coach repeated, "Which one of the Ten Commandments is okay to break or ignore?"

In almost unison, our group strongly responded, "None of them!"

With a stern face, he then challenged, "If you really believe that, then when was the last time you went a full 24 hours without checking your email? When was the last time you turned off your work phone?"

A tense silence fell over the room. Nobody replied; nobody moved.

Our coach then shook his head and shouted, "You are sinning! Don't come back to this network until you deal with that sin!"

The whole room was speechless.

What an eye-opening experience this was for me!

From that time forward, I started a journey by first confessing my sin of not honoring the Sabbath. Second, since I must work on Sundays, I began consistently observing the Sabbath on another day of the week. Finally, I started examining my life for any positive or negative effects connected to taking a day each week to rest, and what I discovered gave me a life-changing "Ah-ha" moment.

Suddenly, I didn't feel as stressed out as I had for so long. Each week I observed the Sabbath, I could literally feel my anxiety level drop to a much more manageable level. I kicked myself as I realized that I had preached to congregations for years to honor the Sabbath, and yet by not doing so myself, I had created unnecessary anxiety and stress in my life. I've learned the hard way that when I break the Ten Commandments, I break myself.

Of course, our modern culture frequently ignores the Ten Commandments, especially the Sabbath. Modern society says that everything should be available 24 hours a day, 7 days a week, every week of the year. Our culture says that we should go and go and go until we can't go any further. Even on vacation—which most people say is for rest—we are encouraged to travel further and participate in even more activities than we would do in a regular work week! You may have even said after returning from a trip, "I need a vacation after my vacation!"

Our culture has forgotten that we need a day of rest. Because we have ignored this commandment, we are literally breaking ourselves down—body, mind, and spirit. If you don't believe me, ask any medical doctor what their number one prescription is. You might think it's an antibiotic or anti-inflammatory, but you'd be wrong.

Doctor's Prescription

One weekend, I was at a men's spiritual retreat. I sat at a table with about 7 other men. One of those men was a doctor. He was a lot of fun to be around, partially because, at this men's retreat, everyone loses their title. You get to be yourself. He was interested in learning about my profession, and I wanted to know more about his.

We both admired each other's jobs because we both cared about people, and we ended up talking a lot during the retreat. During one of these conversations, the doctor leaned over and strangely declared, "Jeff, I get excited when someone comes into my office and says that they have pain in their stomach or leg."

I looked at him curiously. I didn't quite understand where he was going with this statement, so I asked him, "Why?"

He smiled as he replied, "Because about 90% of the people that come into my office say that they feel depressed and down and just need something."

I was shocked! According to this doctor, about *90%* of his patients complained about mysterious physical pains; however, they were really struggling with anxiety or depression mostly brought on by stress.

I believe that we live in a society filled with stressed-out people because we have forgotten to honor the Sabbath by taking a day of rest each week.

I am so grateful for the challenge I received from my network coach and for the confirmation I received from the doctor at the men's retreat. At the time, I was on the edge of burnout myself. I preached 3 times on Sunday, counseled people from my congregation, led my staff, and taught membership classes—all on the same day! Talk about exhausting work.

When I got home Sunday evenings, I'd usually collapse onto my living room couch and then lie there rethinking my day, groaning about mistakes I'd made, and wishing I'd done a better job. I was broken and didn't know how to fix myself. For me, the answer to fix all my problems was to just work harder. But there eventually came a point where I couldn't work any harder.

And that's where I found myself after the men's retreat. I was at a crossroad. I had to make a decision to change my life. I believe that God had been with me all along, nudging me to honor the Sabbath. I believe that He wanted to heal me. So, after discovering my sin and repenting of it, I began to take Fridays as my Sabbath day. Even today, if you were to call my cell phone on a Friday, you'll hear a voicemail that says:

> "Hello, you have reached Jeff Daws. I am sorry I have missed your call. If you leave a message, I will return your call as soon as possible, but not on Friday, for that is my day of rest."

I believe that we must have a spiritual recharging to have the internal strength to fuel a passion for God, perseverance to continue onward, and commitment to stay true to the course. You and I need rest, not just more sleep, but a complete day to forget about work and to focus on God and His love for us. Life is a series of sprints, not a marathon.

Running Fever

I've tried long-distance running myself. In 2010, I started running in my neighborhood as a form of exercise. The route was only a little over 2 miles, and after a few weeks, I was able to run the entire neighborhood without stopping. Suddenly, I had an idea: *What if I ran a 5K?*

A 5K is 3.1 miles, not too much further than I was already used to running. So, being a person who likes fun competition, I invited a group of friends to join me, and we registered for a local 5K.

When the morning of the race arrived, I was surrounded by a large crowd of runners, stretching in every possible way. They were amped up for the race, and so was I! In fact, I had secretly decided that I was going to beat my friends to the finish line.

As I readied with the crowd to launch into the race, my wife Rhonda coached from the sideline, "Jeff, remember *The Tortoise and the Hare*. It's not the one who starts the fastest who always comes in first." I nodded. "Great advice," I thought.

And then the gun went off!

The crowd surged forward. Some people looked like they were running as fast as they could. I, on the other hand, took off slowly, choosing to conserve my energy for the end of the race. I chuckled to myself, "You guys must've never read *The Tortoise and the Hare*!"

But then my friends pulled ahead, too. And they kept getting farther and farther and *farther ahead*, until I couldn't even see them anymore! You see, what I didn't know was that a 5K is NOT a marathon; it's a *sprint*. The way to win a short race is to sprint.

I never caught up to my friends, but I didn't let this get me down. Instead, I continued running and gave myself a new challenge. I decided to sign up to run a half marathon. The half marathon was a big jump up in difficulty from the 5K, and as part of my training, I had to learn how to pace myself. I also discovered an important truth that applies to our lives and to taking a Sabbath Day each week. The truth is that it takes our bodies *longer* to recover from running a long distance.

Has your week felt like a marathon?

Instead of taking time to rest and renew our energy, most of us keep going, without any break from work. We may even take time off from our jobs, but we can easily bring our jobs along with us everywhere we go thanks to smartphone technology.

Unplug Yourself!

How many times have you gone to a restaurant, park, or on a family vacation and your phone went off, harassing you with emails, text messages, and phone calls about matters from work? That's probably not the way you envisioned your time off.

Instead of giving our minds a chance to rest and reset, we allow little pieces of plastic, glass, and electronics to rob of us of our desperately needed mental rest. And when we don't get rest, we get *stressed!*

In the Bible, God says the way to peace is by keeping our mind on Him. Here's how Isaiah 26:3 (NKJV) puts it, "You will keep him in perfect peace, whose mind is stayed on You, because he trusts in You."

From my life's experience, one of the greatest needs in our lives is balancing stress and recovery. Fatigue can produce anxiety, make us irritable, and fill us with self-doubt. If we don't get adequate rest, our bodies will eventually go into a shutdown cycle, effectively *demanding* that we rest. I encourage you not to allow yourself to get to that point of exhaustion. Instead, make weekly rest a high priority in your life. Sprint over a short distance; pace yourself in a marathon.

I heard a story at a time-management seminar that I have never forgotten. There was a small town that had a lot of lumberjacks in their community. The town's people decided to hold a wood chopping contest to see who could chop the most wood in a day's time. People of all ages showed up to take on the challenge. A gun was fired, signaling the start of the competition. As time went by, many of the bystanders started noticing how all the competitors were young men, except for one man who was about twice the age of all the other contestants.

With adrenaline racing through their veins, the young men chopped wood as fast as they could. But they never stopped to rest. The older man handled the competition quite differently. As the lumberjack sat on a tree stump, taking a break, a bystander asked him what he was doing. The lumberjack responded, "I'm sharpening my ax."

The crowd and contestants laughed at him. What could this older man possibly know about beating people half his age? Well, apparently, he knew a lot, because, at the end of the day, when all the chopped wood was counted, the older man was ahead of the rest and by a *large* margin! The older lumberjack, who took many breaks throughout the day, won the contest.

Here's a principle I draw from that story: It's not the person who works the hardest that gets ahead; it's the person who takes time to rest and sharpen their ax.

Consider the profound words of Psalm 23 (NIV):

He makes me lie down in green pastures; He leads me beside still waters. He restores my soul.

In his book *Sabbath*, Wayne Muller looks at this well-known Bible passage and declares that regular pulling away from work is what allows us to passionately reengage with the world around us.

To me, the Bible is clear that, when God designed our bodies, He built in an internal need for peace and rest. For me, this is one of the hardest things to do, but when I fail to do it, I find myself stressed out.

Reading this, you may have wondered if Jesus said anything about the Sabbath. He did! Listen to His words recorded in Mark 2:27 (GNT):

Jesus said, "The Sabbath was made for the good of human beings; they were not made for the Sabbath."

From Jesus' own words, it's clear that God didn't intend the 4th Commandment to be a curse or just another rule to follow. Jesus says that the Sabbath was meant as a gift for all of us to enjoy.

What Should I Do on My Sabbath?

The following are 4 key things that we can all do on the Sabbath to refresh our mind, body, and spirit.

1) Rest

The Sabbath forces us to slow down. Stress never fully goes away, but the Sabbath can give us a 24-hour break from the stress of our lives. I encourage you to turn off *everything* that connects you to work, including cellphones and email, for 24 hours.

2) Change Things Up

Do things that fill you with energy. If you spend most of your week working with your mind, do something instead with your hands. If you normally work with your hands, do something with your mind, like reading a book.

3) Reflect

Reflect back over the previous 7 days and ask yourself, "What are the most important things in my life, and how am I doing with them?"

4) Worship

When it comes to our spiritual life, we're either gaining altitude or losing altitude. We're never just gliding. I recommend spending some time thanking God, out loud or in your mind, and reflecting on Bible passages. This doesn't have to be for hours but needs to be meaningful between you and God. You can also listen to some worship music and meditate on the goodness of God.

Want to know how to renew your mind on the Sabbath? Take a look at what Paul said in Romans 12:2 (NIV):

Do not conform to the pattern of this world, but be transformed by the renewing of your mind. Then you will be able to test and approve what God's will is—his good, pleasing and perfect will.

When you go into your Sabbath Day, your mind will probably be cloudy with cares and concerns of life, but afterward, you'll frequently receive clarity of thought as a blessing.

I truly hope that you will take the Sabbath seriously and make it part of your weekly routine. Through it, you will encounter the rest that Jesus promised in Matthew 11:28-29 (NIV):

Come to me, all you who are weary and burdened, and I will give you rest. Take my yoke upon you and learn from me, for I am gentle and humble in heart, and you will find rest for your souls.

Chapter 4

Put Money Back in Your Pocket

*R*aise your hand if you'd like to have more money in your bank account.

Wow! That's a lot of hands!

You know, I'm always surprised what people share on social media. It seems like they'll reveal anything about their personal relationships, the fight they had with their spouse, the problems at work, pictures of what they're eating, and even status updates when they go to the bathroom! With people so happy to broadcast their private lives to the world and ready to give their opinion on just about any controversial topic, you'd think that talking about money would be easy. And it is—when it's *other* people's money.

Something strange happens when we start talking about *our* money. It's like people suddenly become aware that they're in their underwear on stage in front of a live studio audience being broadcast to the world, and they run off to go hide. Think about it, when was the last time you saw your friends bragging on social media about how much they owe the bank and credit card companies. Probably not very often if ever.

Most of the time, we only realize that people are in dire straits with their money when they have their car repossessed or their home is being foreclosed on. We make money very private—so private that we keep our financial skeletons in the closet, even from our spouse. And *that* decision can come back to haunt us.

One of the leading causes of divorce is... you guessed it, money problems. Money problems frequently evolve into relationship problems. Imagine how many marriages could be saved if people learned to manage their money better!

I grew up poor and experienced firsthand the pain and trouble that poor money management can lead to. Money was a key factor in my father and mother's divorce, and this cloud of poverty lingered over my family for years. It seemed like most of the time we were just scraping by.

You'd think that after seeing all the money problems I saw growing up that I'd be different when I became an adult, but you'd be mistaken. Like I always say, you can't do better or be better until you know better. But I didn't know better.

Tire Money

I'm a hard worker. By the age of 14, I was working my first job and constantly kept moving up to bigger challenges. At 15, I bought my first car with cash, even though I wasn't even old enough to have a driver's license yet!

So far, so good. I was earning an income and paying for my purchases with cash.

Then, I turned 16, got my driver's license, and was ready to burn up the roads of my town in my car. But there were two problems standing between me and the vision I had in my mind of racing around town with music blaring from the radio and the wind whipping through my hair. Problem #1: My car needed insurance. Problem #2: My car needed new tires.

With my job, I could handle the car insurance payment. But at a staggering 1980's price of $200 for a set of tires, I didn't have enough savings to buy them. I was faced with a dilemma. I had a car but couldn't drive it without tires. What could I do?

I went to my father to ask him for advice. He looked at me in thought for a moment. Finally, he told me to get into his truck, and we were off on a trip to find the money for tires.

After a short drive, we pulled up at our small town's bank. I remember looking at how nice the building was, and I knew that there was a lot of money inside—it was a bank after all! Surely they'd see my need for tires and give me some money.

Dad escorted me inside the lobby and over to a loan officer's desk. The two struck up a friendly conversation immediately, so Dad obviously knew this officer well. I could feel excitement building inside of me as the loan officer motioned for us to sit in the polished leather chairs. Things were looking good. I was going to get tires for my car!

My dad leaned forward and said, "My son needs a loan to buy tires for his car, and I want him to build up his credit."

The loan officer happily nodded, opened a desk drawer, and withdrew a set of papers, which he slid across the desk for us to sign.

And with a few flicks of the pen, the deal was done, and I had a promissory note for $250 with a monthly payment of $37.50. I was dancing-on-the-ceiling happy! I practically skipped out of the bank.

I was going to get the tires for my car, and I was finally going to be able to drive!

But what I didn't really understand at the time was that I had just taken on debt. And much worse than that, I had just started a vicious cycle of borrowing, which would repeat over and over for the next 20 years.

Stuck in the Money Trap

After Rhonda and I married, if we needed something, I repeated the money lesson I had learned from buying tires and visited the local bank to borrow money. Being able to break up large purchases into smaller, convenient monthly payments—with interest payments tacked on—was a temptation I couldn't turn down.

My philosophy of money became: "If you want something, go borrow the money and figure out how to pay it back later."

Over time, our house filled with all kinds of things, from furniture to decorations to electronics and clothes. Whatever we wanted, we bought on credit.

But something else also started filling our house: STRESS!

As our loans and credit card bills started growing, I had to find ways to make enough money to pay back our creditors. I started buying used equipment, lawnmowers, vehicles—anything that I could buy at a discount and sell at a higher price. If we had been financially wise, my side business would've been profit right into my bank account. But because of our poor decisions, any money I made from selling just kept our noses right above the waterline.

And then came kids! I love my children and believe that they are a blessing to me. But, my goodness, raising children is expensive! Adding these new costs to our already tight finances meant that we were starting to sink below the water. We were in a cycle of poor financial decisions, and I couldn't see any way out. The tension from all of the worry about how we were going to pay for tomorrow's bills spilled over into many arguments between Rhonda and me. I'd say that about 70% of these fights were directly related to money and the results of our bad financial decisions.

I knew that we needed a way out of this money trap, but no matter who I asked, it seemed that everyone else was living like us and experiencing similar financial woes. I prayed to God that He'd show us a better way to live because I sure wasn't finding it on my own.

Then one day, the beginning of the answer literally walked through my front door!

With a glow of excitement, Rhonda hurried into our house and said, "Jeff, come here! You gotta see this!"

Judging from her tone, I was both curious and concerned. This was obviously something very important, and I went to her immediately.

She continued, "Look! I found this book by a guy named Larry Burkett, and it shows how to manage money." She showed me one book and then produced a thinner, taller book with a glossy cover. "And look, it has a workbook."

I took one book at a time into my hands and flipped through their pages. I had heard of Larry Burkett before and had even listened to a few of his radio programs, but a lot of what he talked about was a bit over my head at the time. I needed something that could take Rhonda and me, step by step, into a new way of managing our money...and now, here I was holding it in my hands!

While I was still in thought, Rhonda shot a serious look at me, one which means that she is rock-solid determined. Pointing to the workbook, she said, "Jeff, I want to teach this program to my Sunday School class. But if I'm going to teach it, that means that *we* need to learn it ourselves and practice it."

I nodded. I realized that this program could be a way to end most of our money fights, and that thought suddenly felt like a spring of hope rising up in me! I knew that we needed to live in a different way—I just didn't know *how*. But now, God had provided the *how*. Rhonda and I just needed to take the time to learn it and apply it consistently in our lives.

And we did! Our lives and relationship began to change in a very positive way as we began to wisely manage our money. And that was also just the first big step. Some years later, we took Dave Ramsey's Financial Peace University program—an excellent step-by-step money management system. By applying his financial system to our lives, we have seen tremendous benefits in our lives. I highly recommend that if you have not taken Financial Peace to do so.

Money impacts our lives and relationships every day. Think about what Jesus says about wealth in Luke 16:11 (NIV):

So if you have not been trustworthy in handling worldly wealth, who will trust you with true riches?

True riches are things that money can't buy—like relationships. I believe this so strongly that when couples come to me wanting me to perform their wedding, I ask them to go through Financial Peace. I strongly believe that getting your finances right will set your heart moving on the path of success.

Getting OUT of the Money Trap

To get you started on a better financial path, I'm giving you some simple steps that you can begin taking today to get out of the money trap. I recommend that you follow these steps up by taking a full program like Dave Ramsey's Financial Peace to maximize your financial future. Hey, it's your future; don't cheat yourself!

1) List All Your Bills on Paper

This is the first step to financial freedom. It may be shocking at first to see everything that you owe, but it can also be tremendously freeing at the same time. Even though you may not consciously know everything that you owe, your unconscious brain knows and will usually worry about it in the background every day. This unknown cloud of debts and responsibilities hovering in the back of your mind increases your anxiety and stress...and you may not even realize it's happening. Instead, having all of your bills written down reduces those phantom fears.

If you are married, this is the first step to getting on the same financial page with your spouse. As a pastor, I frequently hear people complain, "My wife and I are not on the same page with our finances." My reply is, "Well, show me the page! If it is not written down on paper, then there is no page for you and your spouse to be on."

When Rhonda and I sat down for the first time to write down our bills and debts, it was the beginning of us taking back control of our lives through our finances.

Up to that point, Rhonda had been managing our household finances, and I didn't really pay attention to how much we owed. All I knew was that I was working long, hard hours as a pastor and doing additional side jobs to try to get our family financially ahead. So when

I'd want to go out and spend some money, and Rhonda would say that we couldn't because we didn't have the money. I would get furious with her! I'd hotly demand, "What are *you* doing with all *our* money?! I just made *extra money* and gave it to you! We should have plenty!" This was how many of our fights began, and both of us became more and more unhappy with each other because of this routine.

The moment of change began with us sitting at the table and coming completely clean with each other about what we owed. I watched as Rhonda pulled bill after bill from her organizer and placed them on the table. She then added our bank records onto the pile. I remember feeling shocked beyond words at our financial condition. For years, I had an anger building inside of me toward Rhonda because of our money problems, but here I was looking at our checking account statements and seeing that *I was causing* part of our problems!

That day, I turned over my debit card to Rhonda. Why? Because it was a temptation that I could not handle at the time. A little purchase here and a little purchase there, and soon, I was creating a huge problem for both of us. The card had to go.

After figuring out what had to be paid—the necessary expenses like tithing, housing, utilities, food, etc.—and setting aside monthly for them, Rhonda and I looked at what was left over and figured out how much we could spend a week on unnecessary expenses. For us, at that moment in our lives, it was $20 a week for each of us. If I wanted to buy a pack of gum at the gas station, it came from that $20. A stop at a fast-food restaurant? It came from the $20. If Rhonda wanted to go shopping for a new blouse, it came from her $20. I loved to play golf, so I'd have to save up my money to play once a month.

This first step of writing down what we owed and creating a simple budget based on our income and expenses helped reduce tension in our relationship. We signed our simple budget agreeing to stand by it and that we'd both have to agree to any changes to it. Finally, for the first time in our marriage, we felt like we were in this together. We were determined to get out of the money trap, and we eventually did. The great news is that you can, too!

Create a budget. It's simply a plan written on paper that shows where all of your income goes each month. It shows all of your bills and how much their cost is each month. As the month goes by, you write down the money you make and put money on paper toward each bill you have. At the beginning of each month, start over. Rinse and repeat.

Let me tell you, my friend, budgeting has given far more happiness to our marriage than the small amount of work it takes to set up and maintain a budget.

Ready to get on the same page as your spouse? Write down your money plan.

Careful planning puts you ahead in the long run; hurry and scurry puts you further behind. Proverbs 21:5 (MSG)

2) Destroy Your Credit Cards Before They Destroy You

Most people spend more than they make, so by the time they pay their bills and living expenses, they have nothing left over to save. These people have a problem, and the credit card companies are more than happy to offer their credit card as the solution.

Through the years, I've heard people say, "I only use my credit card for emergencies." But the problem that I observe over and over again in these very same people's lives is that just about *anything* can be an emergency! Your refrigerator dies: potential emergency. You want to buy a new big-screen TV: not an emergency. It seems that people can rationalize almost anything into an emergency—and that's financially dangerous.

Many people don't understand that a credit card is an open line of credit. Prior to credit cards, the only way most people could gain credit was through a loan from a bank. Think of all the times you've signed a credit card purchase. You were actually signing a loan, and your signature was your agreement to pay the lender back.

Of course, nowadays, credit card companies spend millions of dollars on advertising to make their cards look like status symbols, used by beautiful and smart people. They push the message that using their card is the intelligent thing to do, that it gives you the financial freedom to do whatever you want, and that you are getting free money. The credit card companies know that when consumers use their cards at stores and don't have to hand over physical money for whatever they're buying, the buyers feel like they're getting stuff for *FREE*.

But that is the trap! Now the shopper wanders around stores and online sites with the idea, "I haven't spent that much; I can just pay for this later." Most people claim to "track" how much they're spending, but when these same people get their credit card statement at the end of the month, most of them squint at the long list of purchases, stare at the grand total owed, and exclaim, "I spent *that much*?!" And then the process repeats month after month, year after year. The interest—which really didn't seem like much at first, only a couple of dollars—grows and grows and grows.

Eventually, many people get to the point where they can only pay the minimum monthly payment on their total credit bill. And THAT is where the credit card company wants you to be. They want you to be stuck in their money trap, paying only the minimum payment, so that interest can compound on your loan over and over, every month. You then become one of the millions of customers handing over your hard-earned money to the credit card companies every month so that they can pay their bills and have beautiful buildings and pay ridiculously high salaries to their leadership. How generous of you! What seemed like a plastic card to freedom has become the chains of financial slavery.

That may be very heavy, but does any of that sound familiar? Let me tell you, I have been there, and there *is* hope!

If you're currently in a credit card mess or see yourself heading in that direction, the following simple steps will help you take back control over your finances and start walking the road to financial freedom.

If you absolutely must have a credit card, write or print out Hebrews 13:5 (GNT) and attach it to the back of your card:

Keep your lives free from the love of money, and be satisfied with what you have.

3) Build an Emergency Fund

Even after Rhonda and I created our budget and stuck to it as much as possible, NOT having an emergency fund set us back time and time again. We had no savings; and this lack of having money in an account that we could pull from when an emergency came up broke our budget numerous times.

And it was hard work for us to stick to the budget at first. Rhonda would be out and see an eye-catching pair of shoes in a store window, but she didn't buy them because she knew that, at that moment, she didn't have any money available for new clothing purchases in the budget. I'd be with a group of pastors at a meeting, and afterward, they'd all want to eat at a somewhat expensive restaurant. I'd have to politely turn down their offer because I knew that at that moment, I didn't have money available in the budget for me to spend on a meal out.

So after working so hard to stick to our budget, a sudden financial emergency felt like a sucker punch and left us sick in the stomach! It's like we had to start over after each emergency. Either our checking account would be low, or we'd have to turn to credit to pay for the expense.

But there is a very easy solution to avoid or lessen the impact of emergencies, and it irritates the fire out of me that I didn't learn it sooner in life!

Dave Ramsey calls this solution an *emergency fund*. Simply put, you set aside a little money from each paycheck to go into a savings account. And you keep doing this until you've saved $500. After $500, you keep adding to the account until it has $1,000. After you've saved $1,000, you continue adding until you've set aside 3-6 months of your expenses.

Simple right? Start small, work toward enough to pay for your living expenses for 3-6 months. Do you see how powerful this could be for your life? Do you see how *freeing* this could be for you?! Imagine, if your vehicle needs new tires, you don't have to panic or go into debt. You just withdraw the money from your emergency fund to pay for the tires, buy new tires, drive away happily, and start rebuilding your emergency fund with your next paycheck.

Listen. Emergencies happen, my friend! They are a part of life, and according to Murphy's Law, they frequently happen when you least expect them or want them. But how would you feel if the next time one came up, you just withdrew the money from your emergency fund and paid the bill? Simple. Done. Life moves on.

Do you see how this could change your life for good?

And you can get really creative at building up your emergency fund. For instance, Rhonda and I went through our house, gathered a whole bunch of stuff that we didn't need or use, and held a yard sale. I had an old Model T go-cart that I was going to restore and never got around to it. Instead of letting it just sit there, taking up space at my house, I sold it and put the money into our emergency fund.

In less than one month, we had $1,000 in our emergency fund! Now, that may not sound like a lot of money to you, but at that time, it might as well have been a million dollars, because it made both of us feel so good to know that we had it set aside in a savings account, ready to use in case a real emergency happened. No longer did we have to run to the bank or a credit card company for help when unexpected expenses appeared. Creating an emergency fund was one of the most important steps that we've taken to financial freedom, and you can take that step, too!

I challenge you to start saving up $1,000 in an emergency fund.

4) Discipline Yourself in Small Financial Ways

How would you react if I told you that the small things really add up, especially when it comes to your finances? You might nod in agreement. You might say, "Jeff, that sounds good, but I don't think it really matters to my finances." Well, how would you react if I told you that you could pay off BIG debt and improve your overall financial situation by being disciplined about small changes?

In addition to creating and sticking to a monthly budget and building up an emergency fund, Rhonda and I followed the small steps that I'm about to share with you, and by so doing, we paid off more than *$30,000* in debt in only *18 months!*

Want to know how we did it?

Here's what we did.

Small Discipline #1: Don't add any new debt

When a bleeding person comes into the emergency room at a hospital, one of the first things the medical professionals will do is try to stop the bleeding. Uncontrolled bleeding will hamper any other efforts to help the patient. This same concept is true in regards to your finances.

If your bank account is hemorrhaging out money every month to pay creditors and bills, you have to stop the bleeding by NOT taking on any new debt. And I'm not just talking about getting a loan for a new vehicle (which you should know is a terrible idea if you're in a financial crisis). I'm also talking about random shopping trips to physical and online stores whenever you're bored or stressed. I shake my head when I hear someone calling shopping *retail therapy*, especially when they are in bad financial shape. Frequently eating out—which is a whole lot more expensive than we usually want to admit—is another common budget buster.

If you're like a typical American, you've bought a $15 pizza with a credit card at some point in your life. Now, there are lots of good people out there who make this SMALL purchase every week, usually on the weekend, with a card that already has a high balance on it. They can't pay off the balance, so they just pay the minimum monthly payment. The interest continues compounding silently in the background, and the real cost of those $15 pizzas, which have been eaten and forgotten, continues growing. It turns the stomach to think that years later, if the borrower continues just making the minimum payments on that credit card account, one $15 pizza a week could end up costing them *TENS of THOUSANDS* of dollars!

I don't know about you, but hearing that takes my appetite away.

Small things, over time, have the potential to make or break you financially. Don't add ANY new debt, no matter how small, if you're trying to get out of debt.

Small Discipline #2: Cut back on monthly bills

When I went through Financial Peace, I heard the testimonies of people who paid off $30-40,000 of debt in less than 24 months, and I didn't believe it. To me, it seemed too good to be true. I also thought that those people must've gotten a big inheritance, bonus at work, or sold off their house to pay off that much debt—if what they were saying was really true. I remained skeptical that small changes could have such a big impact on personal finances.

And then Rhonda and I started taking a closer look at our monthly bills.

Do you know what we found? We found $400! Now, you might be confused right now at what I said, thinking, "How do you get money from a bill?" I'll tell you what we did, but first, let me ask you, what could you do with an extra $400 a month? Just think about it for a moment. Think about how much debt you could pay off.

Here's how Rhonda and I turned our bills into extra cash.

We gathered all of our bills together, and one by one, we called each of these companies and renegotiated our services and fees. We also cut out services that we no longer needed.

For example, I had just bought a new cell phone. It was one of the first phones that could receive emails, and I was extraordinarily proud of it! Confession is good for the soul, so I must confess that I loved taking it out in front of people and showing it off. But...with this phone's data plan, it cost me around $65 a month. And thanks to its contract, I couldn't give the phone back to the phone company and downgrade to a cheaper phone. I was stuck.

So what did I do? I reluctantly called customer service and turned off the data. I may have been the only person in the U.S. at that time who owned this popular phone and didn't have data on it, BUT, I had an extra $35 a month in my bank account. That's $420 a year to help pay off debt, and I still had a phone that I could call and text on.

Rhonda and I were on a roll now because we could see that cutting monthly bills put MONEY back into OUR bank account.

We renegotiated our life insurance from a whole life plan to a term life plan and ended up getting more insurance coverage for less money. We cut our cable and internet bill in half by going to the basic package. At first, I was sad that I had to give up my sports channels, but the sound of money going back into my bank account eased my grieving. Eventually, I realized that I could catch up on sports news online for free.

And now that we are out of debt and can afford all the cable we could ever want, we don't even have cable service anymore! I put a small $30 antenna on the back of our house, and we get all the major TV stations in HD for free. Count with me here: That's $75 a month, $900 a year, $4,500 in 5 years, and $9,000 in 10 years that we save by not having cable! Cutting your bills can put some serious cash back into your bank account!

So what bills are you overpaying on? What services do you have just because other people have them? What less expensive options exist that still offer you what you need? Where could you cut to put money back into your bank account? Even the smallest bit you save adds up over time.

5) Start a Debt Snowball

Here's another life-changing practice we learned from Dave Ramsey: the debt snowball. Have you ever made a snowman? Here in Atlanta, if we get half an inch of snow, schools close and work is canceled. Kids go outside and try to make a snowman from the dusting of snow we got. But here's how you make a snowman.

You take a small handful of snow and compress it together to make a snowball. Then, you slowly roll it around on the ground. Of course, here in the South, it picks up more dead grass than snow. Eventually, the snowball gets bigger and bigger. Our miniature southern snowman starts to take shape with a 12-inch base layer, followed by another about 8 inches wide, and finally, the head being about 4 inches. *Tada!* Our mini snowman is complete!

Now, I'm sure that those of you who get plenty of snow each winter have made a life-size snowman at some point in your life. And most of you are probably wondering what in the world snowmen and snowballs have to do with getting out of debt.

The idea is brilliantly simple! Start with your smallest debt. Take the money that you have cut from your bills or earned from an extra source of income and pay down the first debt until it is completely paid off.

Now that you've got the debt snowball rolling, focus on your next debt in size, working from small to large. Add the money you were using to pay off the first debt to what you were already paying monthly on the next one. It's like you're doubling up on this debt.

Once that one is paid off, you move on to the next larger one, until eventually, you've paid off all your debt.

Here's an example of what our debt snowball looked like. We had an orthodontist bill of $3,000, and we were paying $75 a month. We took the extra $400 a month we had cut from our expenses and added it to our orthodontist bill. So now we were paying $475 a month. Within 5 months, we had that bill paid off!

Again, when you are doing the debt snowball, always start with the debt with the least amount, even if it has a low-interest rate. The reason to start small is that it gives you a win when you pay it off. A small win helps you stay focused to keep rolling the snowball.

After we paid off the orthodontist, we took the $475 a month and added it toward my car payment of $350. At this point, we were paying $825 a month on my car loan and finished paying it off within a year. Rhonda's SUV loan was next. We had financed for 6 years to get the payment where we could afford it. We then took the $825 extra we had and added it to the $450 a month we were paying for the SUV's loan. Now we were paying $1,275 a month, and because we had already been paying on it for 3 years, we were able to pay it off in about 8 months. Finally, after 18 months, this debt snowball strategy helped us pay off $30,000 in debt! Our last debt was our house, and we've already started working on paying it down.

I shake my head, marveling at how powerful the debt snowball strategy is. And you can do this! It's not rocket science, my friend! It's simple discipline.

Small decisions today equal big outcomes in the future.

Whoever is faithful in small matters will be faithful in large ones; whoever is dishonest in small matters will be dishonest in large ones. Luke 16:10 (GNT)

And let us not get tired of doing what is right, for after a while we will reap a harvest of blessing if we don't get discouraged and give up. Galatians 6:9 (TLB)

6) Start Paying God and Yourself First

I call this important step the 10/10/80 plan. To follow it, take the first 10% of your income and give it to God through your local church. This is called a *tithe*—literally a tenth. Putting God first by giving Him a tithe may seem strange, especially if you've never attended church. For a Christ-follower, tithing is the first step to get out of debt, not the last. Consider what Malachi 3:10 (NIV) says:

Bring the whole tithe into the storehouse, that there may be food in my house. Test me in this," says the LORD Almighty, "and see if I will not throw open the floodgates of heaven and pour out so much blessing that there will not be room enough to store it.

Understanding the Spiritual Implication of the Tithe

God Requires the First 10%

I believe that the first thing to leave your bank account after you've been paid should be your tithe. Imagine yourself holding 10 one-dollar bills in your hand. Then a friend walks up and asks you, "Hey, which one of those one-dollar bills is your tithe?" The answer is the first one that leaves your hand.

The Bible calls this a *first fruit*. In years past, farmers would bring the very first fruit, vegetables, and grain from their harvest and give it to God. An amazing thing about God, though, is that He doesn't just expect you to give. He promises that, if you do, He will bless you and that the blessings will be great. Skeptical? Take a look at the following promise from Proverbs 3:9-10 (NIV):

> Honor the LORD with your wealth, with the first fruits of all your crops; then your barns will be filled to overflowing, and your vats will brim over with new wine.

Did you see in your mind the vivid picture of how much God wants to bless you for being obedient? A barn filled to the point that its beams are splitting open from the weight of the blessings inside! A reservoir, overflowing its banks with blessings that rush all over the surrounding land! With a promise like that, what have you got to lose?

Now, after being a pastor for years, I've observed over and over that it's not necessarily that people don't want to give to God through tithing. The problem is that they wait to tithe *last*, after they have paid out their bills.

I can't tell you the number of times that I've heard someone say, "Jeff, I'd love to tithe, but I don't ever have any money left over after paying my bills." I find it mindboggling that most of these people have no problem spending money on eating out frequently, buying movie and sports tickets, and shopping for new clothes and the latest gadgets. But suddenly, when it comes to tithing—one of the few things that God gives an iron-clad *promise* of bountiful blessing to—these same people are suddenly out of money. I've heard people say, "Oh well, I'll tithe next week." Of course, by the time next week rolls along, they wait to the last minute to tithe, and there's nothing left for them to give.

Give your tithe FIRST, when there's still plenty of money in your bank account, and then see how God blesses your remaining money over time. I promise you, because I've seen it countless times in my life and the lives of so many, that you will be shocked and joyously surprised by how God blesses you when you consistently tithe. Don't wait till next week; make tithing a priority now!

Not Tithing Leaves an *Absence* of God's Best Blessings

Yikes! After talking about how God wants to prosper you through tithing, the opposite is not very pleasant to talk about. I'm not saying that God curses people who don't tithe; I don't believe that at all; and I don't believe that the Bible says that either.

What I do believe and have seen in people's lives is that *not* tithing interferes with how God blesses them. It's like a farmer who picks a few early tomatoes off the vine and then leaves the bountiful, deliciously ripened harvest to rot and wither away. If you're not tithing regularly, those rotting tomatoes were your blessing. God wanted to give them to you, but you chose to cut your blessing off by deciding not to tithe. This may sound harsh, but the wise will read this and say, "Hey, if I start tithing now, it'll open up a whole new field of blessings for me for the rest of my life! What am I waiting for?!" Are you wise?

Give Your Tithe to Your Local Church

When you give your tithe, God is very specific about where to give it to. The Bible calls this place of giving the *storehouse*, which referred to the Temple in Jerusalem. Years ago, the Temple was the central location for worshiping God. People came from far away just to bring their tithes and offerings as a way to worship God.

Today, the Jerusalem Temple is long gone—destroyed when the Roman army sacked the city in 70 AD. Without a central storehouse, the local gatherings of believers, which eventually developed into churches, became the storehouse. One person alone doesn't have enough money to support the many things that God would like to do within a community, but the giving of many believers can transform entire communities.

In most places in the world, the government and private companies do not fund churches. The vast majority of churches are solely funded by those who tithe. Therefore, in order to keep the local church growing, so that its outreaches and message of hope through Jesus Christ continues to spread through the community, its attenders need to tithe regularly. And when you give your tithe to the church, you are giving it to God, and as we've already seen earlier, He promises to bless those who give.

> Bring the whole tithe into the storehouse, that there may be food in my house... Malachi 3:10 (NIV)

The "food" mentioned in this verse is providing what is needed so that the message of God's transforming Word can be shared. Here in the U.S., it would be difficult to attract people to attend a church that had a rundown building, with a leaky roof and peeling paint, no AC or heat, no water, and no leadership to give their best work throughout the week to make each Sunday service as excellent and meaningful as possible. All of those things cost money. So no tithe = no church! Jesus even commented on this topic when he was asked about paying taxes. He said in Matthew 22:21 (NIV):

"Give back to Caesar what is Caesar's and to God what is God's."

Tithing Brings God's Protection

We live in a world tarnished by greed. Sadly, there are people out there who love to take other people's things. No matter where you live, some degree of crime is always present in the region. Don't believe me? Just watch the evening local news.

But I do not want to scare you or emphasize the negative. I want to EMPHASIZE the positive promise of protection that God makes to those who tithe. Never heard of this? Read it for yourself in Malachi 3:11 (KJV):

And I will rebuke the devourer for your sakes, and he shall not destroy the fruits of your ground.

In this verse, the *devourer* is another name for the devil and for those who act like him, stealing, killing, and destroying. For the tither, God promises to *rebuke*, or strongly prevent, any attempts of the enemy from trying to take from you.

Reading this verse, you may say, *"Fruit of the ground?* I don't have a garden. Why is this important to me?" For a farmer, the most important thing for their livelihood is their crop. A rotten or stolen crop means no money. No money means no way to pay bills. And not being able to pay the bills means a whole lot of problems! So what is God promising here in this verse? He's saying that He will protect what is valuable to us. He's saying that He will guard our livelihood. He's saying that He will give tithers an extra layer of divine protection and blessing that other people don't get.

Solomon, one of the wisest men to ever live, understood this amazing promise and wrote in Proverbs 3:9,10 (TLB):

Honor the Lord by giving him the first part of all your income, and he will fill your barns with wheat and barley and overflow your wine vats with the finest wines.

Again, this is not rocket science, my friend! You don't need a Doctorate in Physics to understand this promise. Tithe regularly, and God will bless you mightily! God's Spirit-controlled giving brings God's Spirit-controlled living.

The Tithe Is a "God Test!"

Did you know that there is only one place in the Bible where God asks us to *test Him*? Here, check out Malachi 3:10 (NIV) again:

"Test me in this," says the LORD Almighty, "and see if I will not throw open the floodgates of heaven and pour out so much blessing that there will not be room enough to store it."

Usually, people think about God testing them in their lives to see where their loyalties lie. But in this verse, God explicitly says to test Him to see if He will bless you when you regularly tithe. A key part of this test is that we must give *first*, before the blessings come. Our giving becomes an act of faith. Every time we give ahead of our blessing, we are saying, "God, I trust You." And you could also add to that statement, "I accept Your challenge to test You."

Harold Adams, a man who has attended SCC for years and who played a key role in keeping the church alive when it went through a tough time in the 80s, told me an important life lesson he learned. He said, "Jeff, when I was younger, I worked three jobs trying to have enough to feed my family because no one had ever taught me about tithing."

He cleared his throat and continued. "But I started reading the Bible and learned about giving my tithe back to God. After giving my tithe, I was able to quit two of those jobs!" With a gracious smile and eyes locked on mine, he exclaimed, "God can help me go farther on 90% than I ever could on 100% of my income!"

Human logic says that we can do more with 100% than with 90%; however, God's logic is much higher than we can comprehend. Just like Jesus multiplied a few fish and pieces of bread to feed 5,000—something human logic says is impossible—God can take the 90% of the money you have left over after tithing and multiply it in ways you can't even imagine!

And if you're still on the fence about tithing, think about this: The God of the whole universe keeps His promises. If you are faithful to Him with your giving, He's given you a rock-solid, unbreakable, extraordinary promise to bless you in return. God keeps His promises.

So why hesitate? Test Him!

The Tithe Challenge

At our church, we offer something called "The Tithe Challenge." We challenge people to tithe regularly for 90 days, and we give them a money-back guarantee. Here's how it works: If at the end of those 90 days anyone who has regularly tithed says that they haven't seen any blessings in their life during that 90 days, we refund their giving.

Skeptics reading this may wonder, "Are you *really* going to give a person's money back if they ask for it?" My answer is YES, with no hesitation. You may wonder how we could make such a large guarantee. My answer is simple: God keeps His promise and blesses the tithers!

We've been offering The Tithe Challenge for years now. Thousands have taken the challenge, and the blessings that they have reported amaze me! In all the years we've given this challenge, we've only had one person ask for their money back. *One*, that's it!

Now, we can only offer the 90-day guarantee to people who attend and tithe at our church. But even if you live far away, I encourage you to find a local church to attend and to tithe there and to watch what God does for you. God's track record of keeping His promises cannot be compared to anything else in this world. You have little to lose and much to gain. You won't find a risk-to-reward ratio like this anywhere in this world!

So what are you waiting for? Start tithing!

Chapter 5

To Be Better, You Have to Know Better

$\mathcal{A}$ few years ago, I was thinking about the young people of our community and how some were making bad choices. After listening to many of their life stories, I noticed a pattern that kept popping up. It seems that many of the younger generations have no mentors. Because most families in the U.S. now live scattered all over the country, many children and teenagers grow up living far away from their grandparents and one or both of their parents, and that's sad, because both the adults and the children are missing out on priceless interactions and the passing down of wisdom and values from one generation to the next. A person can't do better or be better until they know better.

Growing up, if I wanted to find out how to do something, I had to ask an adult or visit a library and hope that they had a book on the subject. Now, of course, we have a tremendous amount of human knowledge at our fingertips through the internet. I actually liked it better when my kids didn't have the internet on their phones. I could tell them something, and they would just listen to me. Now when I say something like, "The sky is blue," they'll roll their eyes, tap on their phone, and start reading from some website about how the sky isn't really blue but is violet, but our eyes see blue because of the way light scatters and the way our eyes see color, and blah, blah, blah—as if they were the one who wrote the article to begin with. Sometimes, I really miss the days before the internet.

Broken Brake Light

But the internet is great, too. I needed to replace a brake light in my car and had no clue how to take apart the brake light assembly. But I would not be discouraged! There's nothing that can't be fixed with the right tool—or so I thought. With Rhonda somewhat skeptical at how this was going to turn out, I whipped out a tool belt and started prying at and jimmying plastic pieces that were fitted so snugly, I couldn't get anything to budge.

After about an hour of wasted effort, I finally threw down my tools in frustration and snarled, "Fine! I'll look it up on YouTube!"

And sure enough, a few key taps later, and I had the exact how-to video I needed! I followed the instructions step-by-step, and after completing the job, I admired my work. With my chest proudly stuck out and victory glowing on my face, I strutted back into the house and announced, in a Rocky Balboa voice, *"Yo, Rhonda!* I did it!"

We don't have an information problem today; we have a priority problem. In order to live a fulfilling life, I believe that we have to get to know the Designer of Life: God. Throughout the ages, it has been the role of the parents to pass on a knowledge of God and a love for serving Him to their children, and it has been the role of the grandparents to act as mentors of wisdom and knowledge to their grandchildren.

Today in the U.S., however, there is such a disconnect in families. Without mentoring from their grandparents or parents, many regular American children will grow up uncertain about whose morals and values to live by. And with adults attending church less, more and more American children are being raised without any kind of Christian influence in their lives. They know nothing about the Bible, nothing about its rules for living, and nothing about its promises for blessings from God. According to recent surveys, an overwhelming majority of Americans still believe that a god exists, but they don't which one to serve.

Well, I believe without a doubt that there is a God—the God of Abraham, Isaac, and Jacob—and I believe that He cares for us greatly. And I believe that it is only by living by the principles of the Bible and serving God that we can have an opportunity for a better life here in this world, as well as an even greater life after death.

But life here can be so much better. As a person starts to develop a relationship with God and begins applying the wisdom of the Bible to their lives, they can begin walking as a better, happier, more successful version of themselves. Even when the Bible disagrees with whatever current culture says should be the norm, you can anchor your personal faith in God by knowing that the Bible has survived over 2,000 years, despite countless concentrated efforts to completely destroy every copy of it!

Every attempt to disprove it, discredit it, discard it, and destroy the Bible has backfired, and there are more Bibles in existence today than ever in history! The Bible is God's Word—a letter of love and hope to a world that is drowning in despair. Great civilizations and empires have come and gone and been forgotten, but God's Word still remains and will always remain.

Curious about what's inside this book that has been banned and burned throughout the centuries? I challenge you to examine it for yourself. Grab a copy, open it, and start reading.

You can't be better or do better until you know better.

No Book Like It!

The Bible is an extraordinary book and has distinguished itself among all ancient and present literature. As you read the Bible and listen to its story, you may not even realize that it was written by 40 authors, each of which contributed at least one book in the Bible and some of them several. For the Christ-follower, its message describes God's plan of redemption through the death and resurrection of Jesus and the promise of Jesus' return.

Over a time span of roughly 2,000 years and in a total of 3 languages, each author wrote as the Holy Spirit inspired them to convey the message of God to the people. Even more fascinating to me is that God used all kinds of people to write this book. The authors came from various social standings and with all levels of education, from shepherds to scholars, fishermen and prophets, soldiers and priests, cupbearer and kings. In spite of the stark differences among the authors, the message of the Bible remains remarkably consistent and vibrant. The Bible is a living book, which has the power to speak to you wherever you are in life and in whatever condition you find yourself. Look at how Paul describes the Bible's amazing supernatural inspiration in 2 Timothy 3:16-17 (NIV):

All Scripture is God-breathed and is useful for teaching, rebuking, correcting and training in righteousness, so that the servant of God may be thoroughly equipped for every good work.

"God-breathed"

The Bible is "God-breathed," but what does that mean? *God-breathed*. Let me help you understand. When we talk, air exhales from our lungs and passes through our vocal cords. Using the muscles in our throats, we form sounds, which become words. Our words are literally breath.

In a similar manner, God's Holy Spirit moved through the writers, like air through our vocal cords, to create the words, sentences, paragraphs, and books which form the Bible. Hebrews 4:12 (NLT) says:

For the word of God is alive and powerful. It is sharper than the sharpest two-edged sword, cutting between soul and spirit, between joint and marrow. It exposes our innermost thoughts and desires.

Just as we associate breath with life, the Bible is a living document. According to Genesis, when God created Adam, He formed Adam from the dust of the earth, but it wasn't until God breathed into Adam that the first human became a living being. The same thing happens when a person reads and studies the Bible on a regular basis. It is like God is breathing into that person the breath of life. It gives you the spiritual breath you need from God to make you alive in Him. It is God's Word that breathes God's Spirit into our lives that we may walk in the Spirit and not fulfill the lust of the flesh, which leads us to a life of destruction.

I would encourage you to catch a "God breath" every day from God's Word.

Warning

When you read God's Word, it speaks to the things in our lives that are out of God's will and that will bring us harm. A *rebuke* is God's way of warning us. It's like saying, "What you are thinking or doing is not right and will cause you harm." It is like a parent who rebukes their child for playing in a four-lane highway by saying, "What were you thinking?! Don't you know you could've gotten hurt or killed?!" Here's an example from Romans 6:23 (NIV) of God rebuking us like parents who want the best for their children:

> For the wages of sin is death, but the gift of God is eternal life in Christ Jesus our Lord.

Wages are something that you earn. When you go to school, you earn a grade by your willingness to apply yourself. When you go to work, you earn a wage that gives you income to live. If you ignore God's Word and do the things that He warns you not to do, the end result will be death—but more than just death in this world.

The "death" being referred to in this verse is eternal punishment. God wants us to be able to escape such a horror and has extended the gift of eternal life in Jesus Christ through salvation. He wants to get us going in a direction that will bring life.

Course Correction

The Bible not only warns us when we are going down the wrong road through a rebuke; it also corrects us in our thinking about right and wrong as we live our lives. We all have a tendency to drift off track in our lives. We start thinking thoughts we shouldn't, which leads to saying and doing things we shouldn't. Big problems start off as little problems. Reading the Bible daily helps us to notice these little problems and stop them before they become a monstrous mess. God's Word is like having guardrails in your life to keep you on the right track

I have a friend named Daryl Chandler, who has spent years in the military, and he taught me a word that the military uses: *azimuth*. When soldiers are out in the field and have to traverse unknown territory to a specific location, they start by pulling out their compass to find north. Then, they set a course to get to their destination and launch off on their mission.

However, every person who tries to walk in a straight line runs into the same problem: it's practically impossible over a great distance! Because of terrain variations and obstacles and because every person favors one foot over the other, everyone will naturally drift to the right or left. Before long, the person can be way off track, if not for the concept of azimuth. A trained soldier will stop and check their azimuth after so many paces. By not taking the time to stop and check their azimuth, soldiers have wandered unwittingly right into enemy camps!

How could we apply the azimuth concept to our lives? Check out Psalm 119:105 (NLT):

> Your word is a lamp to guide my feet and a light
> for my path.

Taking time each day to read and reflect on God's Word—even just for 10 minutes—is like our azimuth check. Doing so helps us stay on track by giving us the correction we need on life's journey. Let's face it: We all have a natural drift to go back to our old patterns of behavior. I've watched many people come to Christ and surrender their lives to God for a time. Then, they got busy doing life and forgot about God's Word. Eventually, they drifted back to their old lifestyles and found themselves in a deep mess, wondering how they ended up lost on the journey of life.

Don't let this be you! Take time each day to do a spiritual azimuth check by letting the Bible correct your path.

The How-to Book

The Bible is our moral compass to guide us in the right way of living, but many people look at the Bible as the "No Book." They see passages like the Ten Commandments as interfering with their freedom to choose to live how they want.

I, on the other hand, would say the Bible is the *How-to Book*. It teaches us how to live a life pleasing to God, in which He prospers us according to His promises. Living this way frees us from regret and shame. Think about it: If the deep-thinking God of the universe, who designed every level of existence with infinite creativity and order, expected us to follow some kind of code for life, wouldn't He somehow provide these instructions to us? Wouldn't He somehow bridge the gap between the natural and supernatural to transmit to us a moral code to live by?

Well, my friend, if you're an American, chances are high that you *already have* this divine letter sent from God to all humanity riding around in your car, baking in the sun, or lying on a shelf at home, collecting dust. To me, it's an outrageous shame that the greatest written treasure chest of wisdom for life is left by so many people, untouched, decorating a coffee table.

God uses our reading of the Bible to give us training in the right way of living. Growing up, we learn almost everything about how to live in this world from other people. We watch our parents, our extended family, our friends, our teachers, television, internet, movies, and so on. That conglomeration of information has influenced us and helped shape who we are.

Some of the things we don't like about ourselves, we pick up from others unintentionally. Has someone ever sneered, "You're just like your mother," or "You're just like your father?" Many of us cringe when we hear this comparison, especially if it's a negative trait being highlighted.

But more often than not, if we're honest, it may be true. Why? Because more is caught than taught in our lives. We have a strong tendency to take on the ideas, beliefs, and behaviors of the people around us.

Have you ever heard someone say that their family is cursed with bad tempers, alcoholism, or drug addiction? "Family curses" are actually *bad habits* that have been modeled and passed on from generation to generation. But the good news is that these habits can be broken through the wisdom and power of following the teachings of the Bible.

God's Word trains us or retrains us in the right way to live. Getting God's Word in your daily life brings with it the transforming power of the Holy Spirit to make yourself into a new person. You have to change your mindset to change your life. That's why the Bible says in Romans 12:2 (NLT)*:*

Don't copy the behavior and customs of this world, but let God transform you into a new person by changing the way you think.

Then you will learn to know God's will for you, which is good and pleasing and perfect.

That Piece of Cake

Have you ever tried to change a habit by willpower alone? For instance, you may have started off your day with the noble goal to only eat healthy food all day. With incredible willpower, you had a nutritious shake for breakfast. You powered your way through the munchies with a hand full of carrots. And then lunch rolled around, and you joined some coworkers to eat out. As you stood in line, you may have had every intention to order a salad for lunch, but you found yourself drowning in the enticing smell of fried chicken and French fries; and before you even realized it, you were ordering the fried-meal special!

I've done that many times before and was very disappointed that my willpower alone wasn't as powerful as I thought. Don't even get me started on my struggle with chocolate cake!

But I learned this lesson about willpower's insufficiency in another way when I purchased a brand-new treadmill.

This treadmill was extremely fancy compared to my old one. Digital buttons and flashing readouts decorated its central console. Just looking at its glistening frame, I knew that fat was going to go flying off my body in record time!

It also had a multitude of preset workouts that focused on specific exercise goals. It had programs to target fat-burning and cardio. Like magic, the treadmill could automatically raise its incline to simulate jogging uphill or speed up the belt to increase running speed.

Out of the box, I was in love with this thing and knew that it was going to be one of the most memorable items I've ever purchased! Well, it *was* memorable, but not for the reason I was expecting!

In my workout outfit, I hopped onto the treadmill, scrolled through a series of programs, found one that would push me to my limit—I wanted a challenge after all—and started running. I'd been using a treadmill for years, so I'd tossed the instruction manual aside. I knew that I could always find it if I really needed it. I mean, what didn't I already know about treadmills anyway?!

The run was great! The belt was so smooth compared to my old one, and the digital display showed me exactly what parts of the track were coming up. And I was flying! I mean, man, *I was FLYING!* With my earbuds pumping away with upbeat music, I hit my top speed of 7 mph and maintained it. I was cruising along, to a thumpin' song, and then the track inclined like I was running up a mountain—and it FELT like I was running up Mt. Everest! *Twice!*

After 20 minutes of this intense workout, I could feel my strength waning, so I manually overrode the workout program to slow the speed. The new motor purred as it gradually slowed to the speed I selected, and I smiled, feeling very satisfied. With my heart-pounding, the workout ended as the belt finally came to a dead stop. I stood in place, taking in some desperately needed air.

But I missed something very important by tossing the manual aside. In my haste to try out my new toy, I didn't realize that, unless you hit the *stop* button, the workout program will automatically *restart* at the beginning of the workout.

While I rested, catching my breath, the treadmill beeped a friendly warning that it was starting again, but I couldn't hear it. I was still jamming out to my exercise playlist!

Shocked beyond words, I suddenly felt the treadmill belt rip out from under my feet! I jerked my head up in horror, looking at all the flashing readouts on the control center, wondering what in the world was happening! In that split second, I had a choice to either run or be thrown against a wall.

So even though I was exhausted and out of breath, you'd better believe that my feet ran like fire as I tried to catch up to the belt's speed! With my eyes frantically searching the console for an OFF button, I called out to God for help, and I finally saw the STOP button. I mashed that button with everything in me and sighed in tremendous relief as the belt started slowing down, before coming to a complete stop.

Quickly, I hopped off that treadmill and gave it a leery glance. Was it trying to kill me?

Of course not! But it taught me two very important lessons that I'm applying to the Bible. First, ignore the instruction manual at all peril! I believe that the Bible is our instruction manual for life, so we shouldn't just toss it aside. We should read it daily and absorb its wisdom.

The second lesson I take from this experience is that manual override only works for so long before autopilot kicks back on. Here I'm referring to the autopilot habits and routines we've already programmed into our minds. We can make short-term changes with our manual override of willpower, but for long-term positive changes, I believe that we need to reprogram our mind's autopilot; and this is done through the transforming power of reading the Bible.

God can help you reprogram your mind to live in a better way. Will you let Him? Will you make Bible reading a daily priority? I dare you to do it!

Faith Builder

So then faith comes by hearing, and hearing by the word of God. Romans 10:17 (NKJV)

By reading the Bible and hearing its principles taught, your faith in God grows. When your faith in God grows, hope comes flooding in. By giving time to God's Word, we are giving time to God Himself. It is through God's Word that He speaks to us, and it is through prayer that we speak to Him. Listening is a necessary part of every growing relationship, and reading the Bible is like we're listening to God speak directly to us in written form.

Personally, my faith grows as a result of getting closer to God by reading the Bible. I gain the confidence to live life with a deeper sense of trust in God as my Heavenly Father.

When I was a little boy, I would help my dad on Saturdays, working in his shop behind our house. After a day's work, my dad would take me down to a local store where he would buy me a Pepsi and a pack of peanuts. We would pour those peanuts into our drinks. I don't know who started this tradition in my family, but that is the way we roll with Pepsi and peanuts.

Sometimes, we would get into my dad's truck to make the trip down to the country store, and he would suddenly stop the truck and say, "Jeff, do you want to drive?"

Now, I'm not advising all you parents out there to do this because of all the obvious safety reasons, but for me as a kid, I was happy as a flea on a dog to be offered an opportunity to drive. I would answer my dad with a resounding, "YES!" and jump into his lap. Dad would put my hands on the steering wheel and control the gas and brake pedal.

Once we began to move, he would take his hands off the wheel and announce, "Jeff, you're driving!" At that moment, I would feel so grown up and in control. As the truck would start to wobble toward the shoulder, Dad would chuckle and say, "Keep it on the road, son."

As long as the road was straight, I was okay driving, but when we came to a curve, I would start to feel panic rising within me. This was all new to me, and I was uncertain about what to do. But before I could say, "Daddy, I can't do this," my dad's arms had already reached around me and were calmly holding the steering wheel. He didn't yell, "Try harder!" He just quietly guided the car through the curve.

My childhood experiences of driving remind me a lot of what it's like to have a growing relationship with God by reading His Word. You learn to trust God to take the steering wheel of your life and to drive you through the places which fill you with so much fear that you don't know what to do. Remember, you can't do better or be better until you know better.

Your opportunity for a better life will come through reading and studying the Bible. Jesus said it this way in Matthew 7:24-26 (NIV):

> "Therefore everyone who hears these words of mine and puts them into practice is like a wise man who built his house on the rock. But everyone who hears these words of mine and does not put them into practice is like a foolish man who built his house on sand."

Over 25 years ago, I began a habit of getting up at 6 a.m. to read God's Word. At first, it wasn't easy. I would've much preferred staying in bed and sleeping longer. But as I have invested this time into being in God's presence and reading His Word, God has blessed me in return over and over, far beyond anything that I could've imagined. This one practice alone has impacted my life more than I can describe in words!

Read the Bible to be wise. Believe it to be safe. Practice it to be holy. I challenge you to go ahead, right now, and pick a time of the day that you'll give 10 minutes to reading the Bible. I promise you that the returns on your investment of time spent with God in Bible reading will be so immense and life-transforming that you'll wonder why you waited so long to start!

Chapter 6

The Power of Forgiveness

I think that one of the hardest yet most freeing things a person can do is to forgive.

When I was a little boy, my mom married a guy who loved to drink alcohol. Because of his addiction to alcohol, my stepfather couldn't keep a steady job, which forced my mom to provide for the whole household—and with 4 children, that was a challenge! I can't even imagine what the pressure was like to carry such a financial burden.

Despite Mom's best efforts, sometimes we'd fall behind on our rent payments and would have to move. When we couldn't find affordable housing, we'd move in with a set of grandparents. My mom did everything she could to hold our family together. She'd already been through one divorce and didn't want to go through it again. But as time went on, my mom and stepfather would argue, and occasionally, those arguments would turn into physical blows. Needless to say, being just a little boy, I was scared that my mom would get really hurt. After a while, that fear began to give way to another emotion: *anger*. The root of anger worked deep into my heart, and I became so furious with my stepfather that I swore I would kill him when I grew up.

My mom endured this toxic relationship, hoping that one day her husband would see the light and change. But as time passed, and she saw how their fighting was hurting her children, she decided that the only hope for us was to end their hopeless marriage.

When I was 11 years old, they divorced. The divorce legally ended their union in the eyes of the state, but it didn't end the bitter rage inside of me. In my mind, I still wanted to physically hurt my stepfather and would lay awake at night, thinking of how I could get even with him for hurting my mother.

After the destruction of their marriage, I didn't see him very much—which was fine by me. As time ticked on, I made the life-changing decision to follow Jesus as my Savior. Nevertheless, the monster of anger still lurked in the shadows of my heart, feeding on my unforgiveness. But it didn't stay hidden in the dark for long.

When I'd least expect it, I'd feel a wave of anger well up inside me and burst out of me in ways that surprised and concerned me. Many times, the very people who I love the most in this world would be on the opposite end of my rage, and I knew that I couldn't let this continue anymore. I decided that I had to get to the bottom of what was causing my rage and defuse this ticking time bomb inside of me.

I thought about seeing a counselor, but I worried about what people would say or think of me. Typically, people tend to think of pastors as being perfect or having no problems. I imagined people from my congregation sneering, "There's that preacher! He's the one that's so jacked up, he has to go see a counselor!"

But I knew I had to do *something*, because doing *nothing* was threatening to destroy my life!

So, I swallowed my pride, faced my fears, and started visiting a Christian counselor. And, oh, what a life-changing decision it was! Over a good period of time, my counselor helped me work through a multi-tude of complications from my past that had unknowingly turned me into a man filled with anger, frustration, anxiety, and fear. In my first sessions, I sat down in the chair and expected my counselor to write up a list of things for me to do that would magically cure my problems, just like a doctor filling out a prescription.

Instead, the counselor helped me examine key events in my life that I was allowing to hold control over me. With God holding one of my hands and my counselor holding the other, they helped me confront the pain of my early life and helped me let go of the rage that I had been bottling up inside me since then.

And I would like to share with you what I learned as I walked the path of forgiveness.

Let go of "having a right" to be an angry person

There is a big difference between getting angry and being angry.

Getting angry is when you've seen or heard something that grabbed your attention and triggers a defensive response in you. It can be positive—you defend yourself or someone else if physically threatened. It can also be negative—someone cut you off in traffic, and you want to get even with them.

Living in anger is walking around with a chip on your shoulder, daring anyone to knock it off. It's like living in a cloud of negative emotion, which everyone around you can feel and dislikes. And it is usually the people that you are closest to who pay the price for your anger.

Anger has been around with humanity since Adam and Eve's fall, and all experience it at times in their lives. But Proverbs 16:32 (ESV) declares that,

Whoever is slow to anger is better than the mighty, and he who rules his spirit than he who takes a city.

A question for you to ask yourself and to answer honestly is, "How long is the fuse that is attached to my anger-dynamite?" Short? Long? Don't know because you never thought about it? Think about it, because it's important that you know about how long you can endure whatever it is that lights your fuse so that you don't blow up, especially on your family, friends, and coworkers.

Do you know what can really make anger grow? It's the desire to get even with someone. The very thing that causes unforgiveness is the very thing that leads to anger. Anger and hate are the emotions we feel when we hold on to the desire for revenge. If you don't let go of wanting to get even, desiring hurt for them, or even praying for God to pay them back, your anger will control you. You are literally choosing to turn over control of yourself to an emotion that can become an uncontrolled monster.

I've seen nicely dressed, professional-looking people lose their temper at airports, restaurants, grocery stores, malls, and golf courses, just to name a few places. One minute, they're the poster child of a successful adult; the next minute, they're acting *like a child*, throwing a tantrum because they can't have their way.

Listen to what Paul says in Ephesians 4:26 (NLT) to all of us:

And "don't sin by letting anger control you." Don't let the sun go down while you are still angry.

When you give control to your anger, you'll do things that you'd never really want to do. Many of the things I've done in my life that I regret I did while I was angry. You can probably think of times in your own life where you lashed out at someone or smashed something because you were furious about something else, and then afterward, you were filled with remorse over what you did.

So what should we embrace instead of anger?

Meekness. Hearing that word, you might think that "meekness" means "weakness;" however, meekness means "control" and actually requires great emotional strength. A horse is an excellent example of meekness. Horses have powerful muscles, allowing them to race at great speeds for hours. But even with their great strength, a child can ride a trained horse, because the horse restrains its power. The child can then steer the horse with thin reins attached to the bit in the horse's mouth.

Meek people are some of the most emotionally strong people in the world. Why? Because they don't just react to whatever their emotions shout to them to do. They think and consider what is going on and seek an alternative solution to the problem without flying off the handle and throwing a tantrum.

I challenge you to practice meekness. Whether you're a person who loses their temper easily or not, meekness takes work, but I'm telling you that it will save you from doing and saying stuff that you'll end up regretting later. Cultivate a meek spirit in your life.

When you stop showing your anger, you'll stop feeling angry

Here's a technique, which I use every week, that you can use to cool down and help avoid arguments. When someone says something to you that requires a response, ask them to give you 24 hours to think about what you've said. By the time 24 hours have passed, you'll be able to process your emotions better and give a response that you won't regret.

As a pastor, I interact with many people throughout the week. Sometimes a person will get angry with me about something I preached and will try to corner me to debate me over their own personal philosophy. Any time I'm put on the spot to give a quick answer—especially when the question is intended to "push my buttons"—I can feel my *pride* sparking defensive anger within me. If I don't rein in my emotions, I know that I can start veering off into the danger zone of anger, and I want to avoid that. Like Proverbs 16:18 (GNT) says,

Pride leads to destruction, and arrogance to downfall.

Instead of standing there and getting into an argument, I ask for 24 hours to think about the question and politely break away from the conversation. Physically moving to a different location helps tell my brain that I'm safe and calms my emotions. Now that I've returned to a calmer state, my brain will quietly process an answer, and the next day, I will know how to respond.

Try out the 24-hour technique. You can use it in any non-emergency situation (and very few things are actual emergency situations). Besides seeing its effectiveness in my life, I've had many tell me that the 24-hour technique is a fantastic argument-preventer in the workplace and at home. So, go on; put this tool in your toolbox and take it out when you need it.

Let it out

Unforgiveness is a tricky creature that convinces you that you're hurting someone who hurt you by NOT forgiving them. But in reality, the person being hurt most is you. Unforgiveness eats away at your heart and your peace of mind, but it can also hurt you physically.

Many people experience issues with their stomach. For some, these issues are not created by an infection or allergy but by bitter unforgiveness. For these, it's not what they're eating that is causing the problem; it's what's *eating them.*

Rick Warren, the pastor of Saddleback Church, often says that, "revealing your feelings is the beginning of your healing." There is much truth in this statement. Many people—especially men—don't like to talk about their feelings. Why? Because in their minds, discussing what they're feeling makes them weak, and I confess that I was like this and still struggle with talking about my emotions.

Interestingly, God says the opposite when He spoke to Paul, as recorded in 2 Corinthians 12:9-10 (NLT):

> My grace is all you need. My power works best in weakness. So now I am glad to boast about my weaknesses, so that the power of Christ can work through me. That's why I take pleasure in my weaknesses, and in the insults, hardships, persecutions, and troubles that I suffer for Christ. For when I am weak, then I am strong.

Listen to that apparent contradiction again: "When I am weak, then I am strong."

The greatest part of forgiveness is letting go of your *unforgiveness.* To start walking the path of forgiveness, I recommend that you find someone who you trust and tell them about what happened and how the other person hurt you. Admitting that something hurt you is being honest with yourself and God. We can't move beyond the pain of our hurts if we constantly say to ourselves, "It doesn't bother me." If you keep lying to yourself, it is a sure sign that something is *really* bothering you.

As a pastor, I get excited when a person says that they want to tell me something they have never told anyone before. It's not that I'm excited to hear what I'm about to hear. Many times, the remembrances these people share are deeply tragic and painful to listen to. What I'm excited about is that I know these people are taking a *bold, brave move to change their lives* and to become free from the oppression of unforgiveness.

It has been said, "You are only as sick as your secrets." I encourage you to find someone this week—a pastor, priest, counselor, or trusted friend to talk to about the burden of unforgiveness you've been carrying so that you can start living a life of freedom.

As my friend Brandon Keller says, "It's okay to have a past, but don't let your past have you."

Change That Channel!

I don't know how your mind works, but with mine, I can be driving along a road, happy as can be, enjoying a sunny day, with my favorite music blaring away, and suddenly, my mind switches gears, and I'm replaying a hurtful interaction I had with someone.

I used to think that in order to forgive someone, I had to forget what they had done to me or said about me. I would try to forget, but the memories would come right back! My friend, if you're struggling with trying to forget, let me encourage you with this truth: Aside from some kind of miracle, it's impossible for us to fully forget what's happened to us. Our minds just don't work that way.

Only God can forgive and forget. Confusing forgiveness with forgetting only interferes with your ability to forgive others and live in peace.

So how can we handle those thoughts of past hurts when they come to mind? I learned from my counselor to *change the channel!* When I say "change the channel," I mean that we choose to start thinking about something else. Consider this verse in Colossians 3:13 (NIV):

> Bear with each other and forgive one another if any of you has a grievance against someone. Forgive as the Lord forgave you.

This verse says to forgive others as God has forgiven you. In order to get our minds off the painful things that have happened to us in our lives, we have to choose to think about what Jesus has done for us. So how do we change the channel? We intentionally remember what God has done *for* us, instead of what someone else has done *to us.*

Anytime you are struggling with the thoughts of hurt from your past, just start thanking Jesus for what He did on the cross by forgiving your sins. If you let your thoughts of hurt become a trigger to help you remember to thank God for his forgiveness, it won't be long until those painful thoughts become weaker and appear less often in your mind. Even when they randomly pop back up, the sting of hurt won't be what it used to be.

I believe this was one of the things that Jesus was trying to teach us in the Lord's Prayer when He said in Matthew 6:23 (NIV),

> And forgive us our debts, as we also have forgiven our debtors.

He emphasizes that when we think about what God has done for us, it enables us to quit thinking about what others have done to us. Change the channel!

Receive God's Forgiveness

You must voluntarily accept God's forgiveness. God can stand at the door of your heart, knocking with the gift of forgiveness in His hands, waiting for you to open the door and let Him come inside with His gift, but until you open that door and accept His forgiveness, you will never be completely free from your past. I've heard many people say that they keep asking God to forgive them for something they did years ago. I listen to them but shake my head inside myself, because they are mis-understanding God's forgiveness.

My friend, if you've accepted Jesus into your heart, you can ask God to forgive you for things in your past and leave them at His feet. A beau-tiful exchange takes place, where God accepts your pains, memories, and failures in exchange for joy, peace, and hope! Receive God's forgiveness!

You may ask, "How do I do this?"

The answer follows!

Understanding God's Forgiveness Means Asking for Forgiveness

But if we confess our sins, he will forgive our sins, because we can trust God to do what is right. He will cleanse us from all the wrongs we have done. 1 John 1:9 (NCV)

Do you like begging? I hate to have to beg someone to do something for me. One of the many amazing things about having a relationship with God is that you DON'T have to beg or bargain with Him!

Does this sound familiar? "God, I will read the Bible every day, the rest of my life if you will just _____." This is bargaining with God, and it's very ineffective. The only thing it brings is more guilt because we make deals we can't keep. So, if you ever find yourself trying to bargain with God, just pray to Him instead. Tell Him in plain words exactly what you're experiencing and that you need help. Don't bargain; ask.

Even with praying and asking God, you may not *feel* any different after seeking His forgiveness. Why? I think we forget forgiveness is about *faith* and *not feeling*. After asking, you must believe that God has forgiven you by faith. His Word says He will forgive you if you just ask from your heart.

It is amazing how many of us believe that Jesus has saved our soul and that when we leave this world, we will go to heaven because Jesus gave us the promise of eternal life through Him. But when it comes to forgiveness, we just can't seem to muster up enough faith to believe that God has forgiven us when we ask.

How do you know your faith is weak in this area of forgiveness? You keep asking God to forgive you for something that happened in your past over and over again. When God forgives you, He doesn't bring it up again...ever. God has the ability to forget what you have done in your past, once you ask him to forgive it.

Imagine God sitting on His throne in heaven, listening to you pray. You ask Him to forgive something that He has already forgiven. I can't say this for certain, but in my mind, I could easily see the Father turning to Jesus to comment, "I have no idea what they are talking about." Here's how Psalm 103:12 (TLB) describes God's ability to forgive sins:

He has removed our sins as far away from us as the east is from the west.

Jesus' suffering and death on the cross opened the door for us to receive salvation and forgiveness of our sins from God. Romans 3:22 (NLT) states:

We are made right with God by placing our faith in Jesus Christ. And this is true for everyone who believes, no matter who we are.

How Does God Forgive Our Sins?

He forgives instantly! The moment we confess what we have done wrong to God and are sorry for it and intend to never do it again, we are forgiven.

He forgives completely! That means that God doesn't hold on to a grudge. If you miss this principle, every time something bad happens to you, you'll think that God is punishing you for a past sin.

All of us have committed sins over and over again. We all have an area of sin that we struggle with and probably will continue to struggle with until we leave this world. When we repent of sin, we have to trust that God forgives us. While praying the Lord's Prayer daily, I lean in on the part that says, "Lead us not into temptation but deliver us from evil." The more I ask God to keep me away from temptation, fewer things of this world catch my eye and interest. We must lean on God's power to deliver us, not just our own willpower.

He forgives freely! Forgiveness is one of your greatest needs. And because Christ died for you, forgiveness is God's greatest gift to you!

Have you asked for and received God's forgiveness? If not, I challenge you to go ahead right now and ask God to forgive you. Afterward, make a choice to start forgiving others.

Forgiveness doesn't erase your past hurt, but it does erase the power it has over you. Forgiveness allows your past to be your past.

Your opportunity for a better life begins developing as you start *livin' forgiven* and forgiving those who do things against you. And that includes everyone—parents, siblings, spouse, children, friends, coworkers, neighbors, people who hate you, people who spitefully try to use you—*everyone*. I recommend that you review these steps daily for the next few weeks and watch how your life gets better!

Forgiven people, forgive people.

Chapter 7

Do Better and Become Better

W hen I became a Christian at 15 years old, I kind of thought that my inner life would become magically fixed by the Holy Spirit. Accepting Jesus as my Lord has been the best decision of my life. But even after my decision, I was still a messed-up teenager with a rough family history, looking for a way to become a better person.

I lacked confidence. I was not a good student in school. I was not the best-looking guy in class. I was not a great athlete. One thing I did excel in was making people laugh, so at school, I used any chance I could get to gain the respect of my peers by being the class clown. My humor may have worked well with my classmates, but in the professional world, it worked against me. I really needed mentoring on how to become a better, purpose-filled version of myself—but at the time, I didn't even know I needed that. All I knew was that I wanted a better life, and I didn't know how to get it. I started the process by giving my life to Jesus, but I didn't know what to do after that.

But God being God, and fully understanding the desire of my heart, connected me with a mentor: my student pastor, Randy Brooks. This man had so much patience working with me. He saw something highly valuable in me that I couldn't see in myself, and he took the time to help me start to see how I could find purpose and a better life by serving God.

At that time, the church I attended had a set of buses that drove routes every Sunday morning to pick up kids to bring them to church. (You may remember me sharing some of my experiences in this bus ministry in Chapter 2.) Every Saturday, Randy and a few volunteers would travel through the neighborhoods close to the church to invite children to come to church.

When Randy invited me to become a part of the Saturday Visitation Team, I wholeheartedly exclaimed, "I'll do it!" In truth, it wasn't that I was super excited to knock on strangers' doors and invite them to church—that part actually scared me a bit. What I was excited about was learning from a person who took a genuine interest in valuing me for who I was and who trained me to become the best person that I could be.

Knock, knock, knock.

That was me, almost every Saturday, knocking on people's front doors. It felt weird at first, but after a while, it just became routine. Soon, Randy promoted me to bus captain, and I finally felt like I was making a difference in other people's lives. It felt so good to do good!

Here's is a great secret of life that I learned during that time:

Your opportunity for a better life comes from *serving others*. You were not created to serve only yourself.

When you hear the word *serve*, what images come to your mind? A server at a restaurant? A person cleaning floors? A worker harvesting crops? A person picking up trash? In English, we have all kinds of negative words associated with serving, including servitude, bondage, and slavery. None of those words have a positive implication, nor are they what I'm talking about when I use the word "serve."

Here's how I define *serving*:

Choosing to do something of your own will to help somebody else without expecting anything in return.

The best example in history of serving other people comes from the life of Jesus—the miracle-working, dead-raising, powerful Son of God, who could call for an army of angels to wipe out a foe but yet chose to humble Himself and even served His own disciples by washing their dirty, disgusting feet. Jesus is our ultimate example of service to the world around us, and He's given us some very important principles to grow by.

1) Focus on others as opposed to just yourself

Jesus said in Luke 9:23-24 (NIV):

Then he (Jesus) said to them all: "Whoever wants to be my disciple must deny themselves and take up their cross daily and follow me."

Jesus' statement to deny ourselves is just as shocking and controversial today as it was back in Jesus' time. I call this life principle, "The Great Reversal." Jesus reversed what the world teaches about finding significance in life.

Our modern American culture promotes finding a better life by making life *all about you*. Don't believe me? Turn on the TV and pay attention to the commercials or study the ads flashed at you while you're on the internet. Advertising is a trillion...*TRILLION* dollar industry, and its sole focus is to convince you that by purchasing a product or service, your life will change forever and you'll feel better about yourself.

Think about it: Is that new miracle sponge going to suddenly make all of your life problems go away? Seriously?! It might help you clean dishes better, but I don't think it's going to help you get a promotion at work or gain self-confidence or pay down your debt or solve your family problems. But when you watched that infomercial, that sponge looked like it magically made all your problems disappear...for $19.99. "But wait! *There's more!*"

I also see this overplaying to a person's *self* in the mentality of our public schools and trendy concepts of parenting. In many of these, *self-esteem* is heralded as a person's key to unlocking success in life. Self-esteem became a big concept in the 1970s onward and expanded into American culture to the point that several generations of youth have been greatly influenced by its philosophy.

Rhonda and I bought into this self-esteem craze when we were raising our children. We tried to do everything we could to make our children feel good about themselves and promote their self-esteem. We were raising young leaders, for goodness sake, so we didn't want them to fail at anything. As time passed, though, it seemed like the more that we invested into building their self-esteem, their self-respect *declined*. Confusing? You'd better believe that Rhonda and I were baffled by what was happening. How could we be doing what the experts championed but get the opposite results of what were promised?

Parents aren't the only ones bewildered by this self-esteem issue. Recently I had a conversation with a college student who I've mentored since he was in the 6th grade. We were riding in my car one day after his first semester of college. He turned to me and said, "Pastor Jeff, your generation has messed up my generation."

At first, I didn't know how to take this statement, but it certainly got my attention. After a pause, I asked him to help me understand what he meant by that comment.

With a shake of his head, he explained, "You guys did everything for us, and by doing that, you've made us think that life would get *easier* as we got out on our own."

He shifted in his seat and continued. "Because your generation did everything for us and made it easy for us, that set up the expectation in our minds that life would be easy; but it's the opposite. Life doesn't get easier when you have to take responsibility for yourself and your actions. It gets harder! We think life is all about us! And then we go to college and work and realize it's not just about us."

He looked over at me with serious eyes. "We can't handle it, man! We can't handle life. We're looking for someone else to do the work for us; we're looking for someone else to rescue us."

He swallowed and waited for another beat before giving me this stunning revelation about the younger generations. He said, "We are full of self-esteem, but we have no *self-respect.*"

Wow, this hit me hard! I started thinking about my own parenting, my own kids, my own childhood, and I soberingly thought, "What have we done?"

The numbers are even more serious. More high school and college-age students are on antidepressants than ever before. For decades, schools have poured money and time into building kids' self-esteem, and yet the suicide rate for children and teenagers has skyrocketed! Obviously, something is not working.

For me, part of this slow tragedy that is unfolding in the lives of young people all across America is that they feel so depressed EVEN THOUGH they literally have a world of endless and astounding opportunities at their feet!

So is self-respect, as my mentee said, a better route for all of us to take? Let's look at Ephesians 2:10 (TLB) for some clarity:

> It is God himself who has made us what we are and given us new lives from Christ Jesus; and long ages ago he planned that we should spend these lives in helping others.

Spend. These lives. In helping. Others. I believe strongly in these words from Ephesians. I believe that God has given us a clear recipe for a purposeful and fulfilling life in these words. I believe that the current philosophy of just feeding a person's *self* creates a famine of purpose and joy.

But after all that heavy talk, I have great news, my friend! We have been given the power to turn this around in our lives by living to serve.

2) Live to serve and not be served

As a teenager, I volunteered for everything that I could possibly do in our church. A lot of times, where I served had nothing to do with what I liked because I certainly didn't like everything I did—changing dirty diapers in the nursery being at the top! But when I did something to help others, I would feel good; I'd feel purpose flowing through my life.

However, serving at home was a different story. I did my chores around our house because I had to. When I volunteered at church, I cleaned the bathroom, mopped the floor, or anything else that needed to be done. But at home, I begrudgingly cleaned those same things.

One day, my dad observed out loud, "Jeff will do anything for someone else, but it's hard to get him to do something for me." Dad was right. At church, it felt rewarding to help people. At home, chores were work!

Have you ever thought of serving as a gift from God? It's certainly a much humbler way of living than the opulent lifestyles of the celebrities and fabulously rich that the media push at us. 1 Peter 4:10 (CEV) says that God blesses everyone with gifts.

Each of you has been blessed with one of God's many wonderful gifts to be used in the service of others. So use your gift well.

I didn't feel like I had much to offer God in service, but I had my hands and a willingness to work. And so, I put these gifts toward helping people. It wasn't long before in our church I moved from being just "Tommy's boy" to forming my own identity. Not only did the people of our church notice what I was doing, but God also took notice. I strongly believe that my willingness to serve is part of the reason God called me to be a pastor.

Throughout my life, I have continued to find great joy by giving part of my life away in serving other people. The world around us says that successful people have other people serve them. But that is not the way it is in God's Kingdom. Jesus modeled God's way to us right after the Last Supper. In John 13:1-5 (TLB), John describes what it was like on the evening before Jesus would begin His journey to the cross..

Jesus knew on the evening of Passover Day that it would be his last night on earth before returning to his Father...And how he loved his disciples! So he got up from the supper table, took off his robe, wrapped a towel around his loins, poured water into a basin, and began to wash the disciples' feet and to wipe them with the towel he had around him.

This passage is mind-blowingly extraordinary! Can you imagine the King of All Existence, taking the time to bow before His disciples to clean their feet? But that's exactly what Jesus did, and His example speaks volumes about how God wants us to live. The world teaches us, "Do something for me, and I'll do something for you." But Jesus shows us to do something for people without expecting anything in return. He laid down His glorious title and picked up a simple towel and began to wash the feet of His followers. For Jesus, the right time to serve people was at *any* time.

To go up in life, I believe that we must be willing to take the time to help people when we see the need. The need is the calling. Jesus said that doing something even as little as offering a person a cup of water was like giving it to Him. It feels good to do good. I leave this thought with a profound promise from Proverbs 11:25 (MSG) that I recommend you write down and put up somewhere in your house, like on your refrigerator or bathroom mirror, so that you'll be reminded of it every day:

The one who blesses others is abundantly blessed; those who help others are helped.

3) Realize you were healed to help

There is an account in the Bible, where one of Jesus' followers, named Peter, had a mother-in-law who lived with him. She was sick and burning up with fever. The fever had caused her to not be able to function, so she ended up in bed in the middle of the day.

Look what happened in Matthew 8:14-16 (CEV):

Jesus went to the home of Peter, where he found that Peter's mother-in-law was sick in bed with fever. He took her by the hand, and the fever left her. Then she got up and served Jesus a meal. That evening many people with demons in them were brought to Jesus. And with only a word he forced out the evil spirits and healed everyone who was sick.

Today, most of us stay away from someone who has a fever because we know that a lot of infections are transferred by touch or through water droplets sneezed and coughed onto surfaces and into the air. I myself am pretty much a germaphobe. I get poked at for the small bottle of hand sanitizer I carry around, hooked to my backpack. So, had I been the one to have walked into Peter's house and found out that his mother-in-law was sick, I probably would've made a polite and quick exit! (Don't judge me here; you know you probably wouldn't want to hang out in a doctor's office during flu season.)

Imagine what's going through Peter's mother-in-law's mind as Jesus comes over, smiles, gently takes her hand, and says, "Get up." If this had been some of us, we probably would've looked at Jesus like He was crazy and said, "What's wrong with you, man?! Can't you see I'm sick?!"

She, on the other hand, responded to His command. And as she did so, she felt the fever break, and her pain subside. Within seconds, strength rushed through her body, followed by wonder and joy at having been healed by Jesus. With excitement, she expressed gratitude for her healing by...get this...*serving* Jesus and the others in the house!

Peter's mother-in-law turned her healing into a way to help other people, and I believe that God wants us to do the same with whatever we've been healed from.

Sin, sickness, addictions, relationship challenges, poor financial decisions, immobilizing fears, anxiety, depression, anger management issues, parenting disasters, lying, cheating, stealing, bad life decisions of every shape and form—these and more are things which plague humanity. If you're a breathing human being, then you have or are currently facing at least one of these things, and it's a serious challenge.

But the good news is that you've also experienced victory at some point in your life over at least one of these and probably many. So what do you do with that victory? What do you do with your healing? Please forgive my passionate excitement about this advice, but I'd shout this answer in reply from the rooftops: "Use your healing to HELP OTHERS get healed!"

The hell you went through in your life is not so that you can look back on it and sigh in relief that you somehow made it through by the skin of your teeth. I believe that God wants you to mine those experiences for golden nuggets of wisdom to share with people who are going through *the same things* that you went through!

As a pastor—having interacted with countless people who were drowning in horrible situations that they may or may not have caused and who couldn't see a way out—I have found that if someone can come along beside them and let them know that they are not alone, it's like throwing out a life preserver called "HOPE" to a person drowning in a sea of sorrows.

My friend, Jesus saves our souls when we follow Him, but that is not where our stories should stop as a Christ-follower. We are healed that we may help others.

So what have you been through in your life? What pain have you experienced? How have you gotten through it? God would like to use those wounds to bring Him glory by helping others get better. I want to challenge you to begin listening to the people around you. Pay attention to those who are going through some of the stuff that you've gone through. Could it be that God has placed you in their path to help them get through what they are going through?

Healing comes when we use our pain to help someone else heal. This seeming contradiction is a beautiful exchange that God set into motion in our world long ago. Look at what Jesus said in Luke 6:38 (NIV):

> "Give, and it will be given to you. A good measure, pressed down, shaken together and running over, will be poured into your lap. For with the measure you use, it will be measured to you."

By helping someone heal, you are deepening your own healing and expanding the ways in which God can use you. I encourage you to get involved in serving at church. It feels good to do good, and it feels great to know that God has used your life to help someone else's life get better. I wonder who will be in heaven, who was on the path to hell, because you took the time to use the pain of your past to help heal the pain of someone else's present.

Chapter 8

You Can Feel Better

*W*hen I married Rhonda, I was 19, and she was 18 when she said, "Yes!" to our wedding vows. Fast forward to today, and I couldn't imagine my own children getting married at that age.

After marrying, we rented a small 3-room house with a tiny bathroom at the back. Our rent was $200 a month, not inexpensive but doable for us at the time. In our small town, the normal routine was to graduate from high school, get a job, and buy a nice car. So that's what Rhonda and I did. Despite having solid transportation, I was always uptight about not having enough money. As I talked about in a previous chapter, our poor financial decisions caused a great deal of stress between Rhonda and me and even threatened to wreck our marriage.

During this time, Rhonda worked at a small furniture and appliance store and could buy things for our house at cost. She never just bought something; she always had a reason in mind when she made a purchase. But, if she did buy something, I would absolutely freak out! And not in a good way!

I had what is called a "scarcity mindset." My mind was consumed with fear that we would never have enough. Now that we have gone through Davey Ramsey's Financial Peace program and put its financial principles into consistent practice, I don't have that mindset anymore.

Because we married so young and knew little about building relationships, we struggled in our marriage. To the outside world, our marriage looked perfect, but behind closed doors, it was anything but that. In hindsight, the two of us just didn't know how to communicate with each other.

What's That Smell?

Have you ever smelled a skunk? Worse, have you ever been sprayed by a skunk? It's a scent so strong that, believe me, you'll never forget it! Well, did you know that there are skunks in relationships? Right now, you might be thinking about someone who you'd definitely call a "skunk" for something they've done. But when a skunk feels threatened, it unleashes a foul odor in order to protect itself.

Guess who was the skunk in my marriage. Who was the person who always seemed to be exploding? Yep, it was me! When I felt threatened or believed that things weren't going my way, I would fire off with a sharp tongue and a loud voice. At that point, I would stink up the whole room with anger.

Rhonda, on the other hand, was what has been called a "turtle." When she was offended, she would go into a "shell" and bottle up her feelings inside. Needless to say, our personality differences and lack of communication created difficulties in our relationship. Probably the two biggest components of our relationship that kept us together over the years were our mutual relationship with *God* and our commitment to *each other*. Though we loved each other, it wasn't the *feeling* of love that kept us together.

My personality type refuses to quit. When we'd have a major disagreement, I would try to show Rhonda love the way *I thought* she would like it. But I was missing her love language completely. One day, we were chatting, and I thought she was hinting to me that she wanted a baby. I thought, "That's the answer! We'll have a baby!" At that time, I was at my first full-time church as a student pastor. With it being a church in a small town, my salary was $17,500 a year, not a lot of money to support a wife and baby. To earn more money for our household, I bought used lawnmowers and fixed them up to sell, much like I had seen my father do as I grew up.

After more talks about having a child, Rhonda and I agreed to try to have a child. And on February 19, 1992, God blessed us with a baby boy, which we named Tyler. I'll never forget the day he was born. First—and this part shocked me to the point of being squeamish—the nurse insisted that I cut the baby's umbilical cord. As I began to cut, I felt like I was cutting off his finger and almost passed out right there in front of the doctor and nurses!

Second, being there with Rhonda and watching as she gave birth to our son was like watching a miracle of God take place! And the moment Tyler was born, something activated in my brain and heart, and I felt an overwhelming love for him, unlike any feeling I had ever experienced in my life! The delivery had been difficult, and Rhonda was completely exhausted from the 12-hour ordeal. I held her hand, thinking, "God, what an amazing woman You have blessed me with!" After the required 3-day hospital stay, we packed up our little bundle—which I fully believed would fix all of our relationship problems—and headed back to our little apartment.

But my expectations of bliss quickly evaporated. Our little bundle of joy didn't like to sleep! As long as someone held him, he would sleep.

But as soon as we put him down, he would start to cry. You may think, "Aww, babies all do that at first." Well, ours decided to do that for *4 years!* Needless to say, a baby didn't fix our relationship problems; he made them even more complicated. During that time, most of Rhonda's attention was focused on caring for the baby, and all of mine was on work. I still found myself scratching my head, seeking an answer to "fix" my marriage. If one baby couldn't make Rhonda and I feel overwhelming love for each other, there had to be another answer to our problem.

As we strolled around in public, I noticed that a lot of couples had more than one child, so I had another "eureka" moment: Let's have another child! Rhonda loves kids and agreed that we should try to have another. Four years later, baby #2 was born! Our precious daughter Katelyn was born, and something extraordinary happened when we got home from the hospital. To our exuberant delight, our son started sleeping all night! Can you hear the "Hallelujah Chorus"? *Hallelujah!* It was a miracle of miracles.

After Katelyn was born, Rhonda and I decided not to have any more children. Rhonda's pregnancy with Katelyn was very difficult, and she almost miscarried. Also during this time, Rhonda saw a doctor and was told that she might have an aggressive form of cancer. I saw myself losing my loving wife and having to raise my children by myself. Those 9 months were a very difficult trial-by-fire.

Despite the turmoil, great news—which I give God complete praise for—followed. Our newly-born, baby girl was a healthy child! And after visiting a different doctor, Rhonda learned that she was *cancer-free!* Praise God! Praise God! *Praise God!* And thankfully, Katelyn was a great sleeper. She'd sleep all night, which meant that Rhonda and I could sleep all night! Hallelujahs again!

Treasure from a Junk Pile

By this point in our lives, I had become the lead pastor of Stockbridge Community Church. In the early days of pastoring SCC, I worked all the time, and Rhonda took care of our children. Our marriage was still not in great shape, but a change was on the way.

One day, Rhonda was sifting through a pile of stuff at the church to see what needed to be discarded or kept, and she stumbled upon some old videotapes of Gary Smalley's teaching on marriage. As she held the thick plastic box of VHS tapes in her hand, she had a genuine *eureka* moment. "Could this be the answer to help our marriage?" she thought.

When she first showed me the tapes she'd found, I was curious but skeptical. But I also thought, "What have I got to lose? Maybe there's something to gain here." So one night at home, we popped the first tape into our VCR and watched it together. Gary shared about how he and his wife had struggled in their marriage and about their realization that they were treating each other the *complete opposite way* of how they needed to act. Suddenly, it was like a light turned on in my mind!

While Gary shared simple, practical things that a husband and wife can do to improve their relationship, I found myself nodding and saying inside, "I can do that." Remember, I said you can't do better or be better until you know better. Through this training series, I began to learn to serve Rhonda instead of expecting her to serve me.

When I moved in with my dad, I saw a picture of what I thought was a great marriage. My dad worked hard all the time, so when he sat down in his recliner, everyone served him. Back then we didn't have remote control televisions. So, if dad wanted to watch another channel, he didn't get up to turn the channel. No! He would call the children from another room and ask us to turn the television for him!

I asked my stepmother one day after I was married why she did everything for my father, and she replied that he worked two jobs and that the least she could do to help him was to serve him when he came home. In her way of showing love, my stepmother was willingly serving my father. But in my marriage, I had been expecting Rhonda to *serve me* without considering her side of the story. In my mind, my hard work was pretty much all the service I needed to give to her.

As we started watching those videotapes of Gary Smalley's teachings, I began to understand that I needed to completely revolutionize the way I thought. The bell sounded loud and clear in my head: *I needed to serve my wife.*

And, my friend, when I began to serve Rhonda, something fantastic happened! Like a young plant, pushing up through the cold ground of early spring, Rhonda began to open up to me, little by little. She began to openly share her feelings with me, feelings which she had repressed for years. And let me tell you, they were *not* all good feelings. But this was an essential part of our marriage's growth!

I'll never forget the first major thing she shared with me as we began to grow. She revealed that for a while, she'd felt like I always put down her ideas and forced mine upon her. For instance, if she was driving the car and I was in the passenger's seat, I would say something like, "Why'd you go this way?!" If she was pulling the car into a parking spot, I would say, "Why don't you park in one a little closer to the entrance?"

Finally, during one of these exchanges, Rhonda had had all she could take and voiced, "Jeff, you're always *correcting* me, and that makes me feel *small*!" Her words hit me like a ton of bricks, which is apparently how mine had been impacting her for 10 years. I never wanted to make her feel bad; I wanted her to feel great. At that moment, I felt sick in my stomach and sad. This was not how I wanted the two of us to live life together.

We both sat there, her words still hanging in the air, my mind thinking of what to say. "I'm sorry," I finally confessed. "I had no idea that I was making you feel this way." I looked at her sincerely. "I'll ask God to forgive me...and I ask you to forgive me. I've been this way all my life, so it's going to take some time for me to change...but...I *will* change." And that was a major turning point in our relationship.

The lesson both of us learned that day was, *"Revealing your feelings is the beginning of healing."* Until Rhonda took the bold step to share how I was making her feel, we couldn't begin healing. Was this a happy day? Oh, no! Not at all! But it was the gateway to happiness in our marriage for both of us.

Is someone in your life currently hurting your feelings? If so, have you told them yet? If you desire to repair or make this relationship better for the long term, you'll have to speak up for yourself and let the other person(s) know the impact that they are having on you. Here's wisdom on this from Ephesians 4:15 (NIV):

Instead, speaking the truth in love, we will grow to become in every respect the mature body of him who is the head, that is, Christ.

According to this verse, when we speak the truth *in love*, we become mature people. We grow up relationally and spiritually!

Our marriage couldn't get better until the two of us learned to communicate with each other and get on the same page. If you want to grow intimacy in your marriage and relationships, "the truth will set you free," as Jesus said in John 8:32 (NIV)—but at first, you might feel miserable. I had to work really hard to change my behavior, and I confess to you, it was a difficult challenge. Rewiring the way you think and act and talk after a lifetime of programming is not easy at all! But, my friend, it's worth it!

With time and God's help, I have changed for the good in many ways—and I *continue* to change, growing myself as I seek to demonstrate my love to Rhonda the way Christ shows His love for His Church.

So how do I continue working on myself and my relationship with Rhonda? At the writing of this book, I have read a book on marriage every year for 10 years. I read the incredible book *The Five Love Languages* by Gary Chapman. I highly recommend that every couple read this book. In it, I learned the mind-blowing truth that the vast majority of spouses want love shown to them in different ways. Without the knowledge of each other's preferred method of showing love, it's like the two people are speaking a different language and neither feel like they're being heard!

But believe it or not, even armed with this wisdom, I still messed up. As I read this book and others, I started to feel like I was the only one working hard to change. I'd gaze up from reading a book and look at Rhonda and wonder what she was doing to make things better for the two of us. I'd read a paragraph in one of these books and say to myself, "Yep, that's Rhonda! *She* should read this book!"

I have to confess to you that I now realize that every time I read one of those books, I was reading it to help me *fix her*. Oh me, oh my! So I would say to Rhonda, "Hey, you need to read this book on marriage." Of course, when someone tries to force something on someone else, resistance is the natural response. But I was determined to breakthrough.

I cleaned the house with Rhonda—something out of character for me in our early years together. I went shopping with her—which at first,

I thought was boring and took way too long. I did these things to invest in our relationship, but again, from my point of view, I saw myself as the only one putting in any effort. I started to get irritated with her. I wondered, "Where is the return on my investment?"

This went on for a while, until one day, I finally had a ground-shaking revelation about myself, the way I thought, and the way I looked at relationships, and let me tell you, I was shaken to my core by it!

The truth is that I looked at all relationships as *trading*. I was good at trading cars, lawnmowers, and old farm tractors. I knew how to buy low and sell high to make a profit. I knew the market cost of what I was selling so that I could protect my own interests. And in trading, you *always expect something in return.*

I realized that I wasn't doing things for Rhonda just to make her happy; I was doing things for her because I wanted affection and attention in return. Because I cleaned the house with her and went shopping with her, I felt she owed me. And it wasn't just Rhonda that I did this to.

I confess to you that I expected *everyone* to return my favors. If I did something for you, then you should do something for me. If you did something for me, I should do something for you. If you bought my lunch today, the next time we had lunch, it would be my turn to buy yours, and if I didn't at least offer to do so, in my mind, I was cheating you.

I'm sorry to say that I even thought this way as I pastored. If I visited people in the hospital, then I felt that they owed me a visit to church. If the church helped you, you should help the church. There were even times that if I had helped someone during the week, I'd make a mental note on Sunday morning to see if they were at church.

Can you see how destructive this way of thinking and living was for me and can be for you? Look at how Jesus teaches on the way we should give in Matthew 10:8 (NIV):

Freely you have received, freely give.

Despite preaching from this passage countless times from the pulpit, I had missed applying it to my whole life. I never freely gave anything and never freely received anything. Even the love of God was not free to me; it was a matter of trading. In my mind, God's love for me was conditional. If I did something wrong, He didn't love me very much. If I did something good, then He loved me a lot.

Have you ever thought that way about God and His love for you?

It wasn't until I was about 38 years old that I began to accept that God loved me, no matter what, and that I could accept His love for me as being freely given.

Counselor? Who Needs a Counselor?!

In my late 30s, I was on the edge of a nervous breakdown. Yes, you read that right. Even though I was serving God, pastoring a church, praying daily, reading the Bible daily, on the road to getting my finances straightened out, and building up my relationship with Rhonda, a series of events, out of my control, threatened to break me apart. A perfect storm hit me in almost every area of my life, and between you and me, I didn't know if I was going to survive it.

In the midst of everything else happening, a family crisis sparked the need for a counselor. I looked for one, and I, being somewhat skeptical of counseling at the time, dismissed the first counselor I interviewed with, and the second one...AND the third one.

I was beginning to think this whole counseling thing was a waste of time. Rhonda and I visited yet *another* counselor to see if he could give us some advice on our family crisis. At the end of the session, as we arose from our seats and started to exit, the counselor said, "I think that everything will eventually be okay..." And then he turned serious eyes upon me and finished his statement with, "...but I'm not so sure about *you*."

His words skewered me right through my heart, and I was furious! Who did this guy think he was to tell me what I needed to do?! I wasn't even seeking counseling for myself! I was trying to help another family member get help! I kicked off the dust of my shoes at that counseling center, determined to never return.

Days, weeks, months ticked by, and the whole time, I felt myself sinking deeper and deeper into a depression that I couldn't seem to pray or sing or read myself out of. I felt like I was falling into a pit without a bottom, and the further I fell, the darker my life seemed to be getting.

Was there a way out?

During this time, the counselor's warning to me kept echoing in my head when I least wanted to listen to it. Every time I thought of his face, standing there in his room, passing what I felt like was judgment upon me, I got angry. And then I reached such a point of overwhelming despair, I thought, "What have I got to lose? He might just help me."

Three months after my initial visit, I made an appointment with the same counselor. When I finally walked back through the door of his office, I announced, "Here I am! Fix me!"

With a laugh, the counselor asked how I was doing, and for the first time in my life, I was absolutely gut-wrenchingly honest with him about how I felt. For so much of my life, I always had to be strong for everyone else, which meant that I stuffed down my emotions deep inside. The traumatic things I witnessed and experienced through life, I stuffed down inside. Misgivings, doubts, fears—everything—I stuffed down deep inside me so that I could carry on with life. But there comes the point in all our lives where the weight of all this is too much to continue carrying alone. We have to share with someone about what we've been through, and a counselor can help you along the path of healing.

During my second counseling session, I brought a notebook with me. I wanted cold, hard-fact answers for my questions, and I was going to write them down and study them when I got home. Thirty minutes into our conversation, my notebook already scrawled with notes, my counselor calmly said, "Jeff, your problem is that you don't trust God or anyone else."

BOOM!

I felt like he hit me between the eyes with a 2x4!

I rose up in my seat to set the story straight and put him in his place. I reminded him that I had been a minister of the Gospel of Jesus Christ for about 15 years and that I prayed every day and that I read my Bible daily. I told him that I had given my life to Jesus Christ as a teenager and that I most certainly believed in God and trusted Him. Who did this guy think he was to tell me that I didn't trust God?!

My counselor remained calmly seated in front of me. In hindsight, I think he may have even grinned slightly. After I finished my defense, he sat silently for a moment, still staring at me, before gently replying, "That's all good, Jeff...But you don't trust God or anyone else."

SMACK!!

His words stung me again! This time I just let the words sink in. As I drove home, replaying the session in my mind, I took an honest look at my life, and to my shock, I realized that my counselor was *right*.

Suddenly, my mindset of trading—expecting to get something when I give something—made sense. Up to that point, so much of life was not based upon faith or trust but upon facts and figures. I didn't trust other people...and I didn't truly trust God. This was going to have to change!

So, I continued the counseling sessions, and my counselor guided me through unpacking how I had developed my way of thinking and treating people. As I shared earlier in this book, my brother died in front of me when I was 6 years old. The counselor shared with me that when that happened, I suffered a traumatic shock, which led to post-traumatic stress syndrome. From then on, I felt an overpowering need to protect myself from anything bad happening to me or anyone that I cared about.

From the time that my brother died until I was in my late 30s, I had a shadowy fear that something was going to happen to me that would violently kill me. Through my life, I would always pray that God's will would be done in every area of my life *except* in my physical life. I would never say, "God, I'm ready to go to heaven anytime You want me." I was secretly terrified that God would say, "Okay! I'll see you in heaven tomorrow."

My distrust of God bled over into all areas of my life. Love cannot grow where there is no trust. Trust is the #1 ingredient of love. Since I didn't trust God, I never really believed deep down in my heart that He loved me. And because I didn't trust Rhonda, I didn't believe that she really loved me.

If love naturally flows from *trust*, that meant I had to try to manufacture it some other way. The only thing from my life-experience that I knew could mimic trust was *trading*, and that was the philosophy I unknowingly chose to live the first part of my life by. Everything in my life was pressure to perform in order to get what I needed most: *love*. But bargaining for love is not real love.

Needless to say, once I discovered the roots of my problems, I began to correct them. I'll never forget the morning I prayed, "Lord God, You can call me to heaven anytime you please. I trust You that You always want what's best for me." Like a new sunrise dawning, I felt like I was starting over with my life. I was actively choosing a different way to live, and I could feel the smog that had been choking my life begin to lift.

When we learn to accept God's love, it inspires us to love and respect ourselves and others. Not only did I learn to trust God, but I also learned to trust that He loved me no matter what. Romans 8:35-39 (NLT) suddenly had such a deeper, fresh meaning to me.

> Can anything ever separate us from Christ's love? Does it mean he no longer loves us if we have trouble or calamity, or are persecuted, or hungry, or destitute, or in danger, or threatened with death? (As the Scriptures say, "For your sake we are killed every day; we are being slaughtered like sheep.") No, despite all these things, overwhelming victory is ours through Christ, who loved us. And I am convinced that nothing can ever separate us from God's love. Neither death nor life, neither angels nor demons, neither our fears for today nor our worries about tomorrow— not even the powers of hell can separate us from God's love. No power in the sky above or in the earth below—indeed, nothing in all creation will ever be able to separate us from the love of God that is revealed in Christ Jesus our Lord.

Every day, as I pray the Lord's Prayer, I say, "Our Father who is in heaven." After I say that phrase, I pause and thank God for His love for me.

Will you receive the unconditional love of God? Will you daily thank God for His perfect love for you? If you do, I am confident that God will breathe new life into you. If there is something in your life that you need to talk to someone about, I encourage to find a close friend or counselor to talk to. The burdens of life can become overwhelming at times. Find someone to share your feelings, concerns, doubts, and fears with. Don't stuff it all down in silence.

Revealing your feelings is the beginning of your healing.

Chapter 9

You Can Live Better

Most of us Americans don't seem to really think of taking care of our bodies as honoring God. When I was growing up, it seemed like everyone kept their bodies in fairly good shape until they got married. After that, most people I knew became overweight. Many of the guys would brag about their enlarging stomachs, as if having a big belly was a great accomplishment. One of my overweight friends worked hard during the day, but as soon as the clock struck leaving time, he was out the door, headed to the nearest buffet.

I'm not making fun of people who are overweight or have a belly—that was *me*, a few years ago. The men in my family carry their weight in the stomach area. Because of genetics, I guess, our stomach is the only thing that seems to collect fat. And the health consequences of this have not been good. I have watched people in my family have open-heart surgery in their 40s. They struggle with type 2 diabetes, heart disease, kidney failure, and loss of sight.

There is a connection between the spiritual and the physical world. When we honor God with our bodies, it is amazing how alive and energized we can feel. Paul reminds us in 1 Corinthians 6:19-20 (NLT):

Don't you realize that your body is the temple of the Holy Spirit, who lives in you and was given to you by God? You do not belong to yourself, for God bought you with a high price. So you must honor God with your body.

As you can see in my family history and perhaps your own, ignoring the truth of this verse can jeopardize your health and happiness. I use the word *happiness* because no one is happy when their health is failing, and they have to live in a doctor's office every week.

I got a firsthand look at what can happen when we ignore the command to honor God with our bodies. My father was going to have some tests done on his heart, and he would not be able to drive back with the medication in his system. So he asked me to give him a ride to his doctor's appointment. I was more than glad to help my dad. At the time, my father was only 49.

After waiting in the office for a while, the nurse escorted us to a treadmill, where she attached electrodes to my dad. While I stood there, I began to look around the room and saw pictures of two hearts on the wall. One picture was of a red heart with all its blood vessels and major arteries. The picture beside it was also a heart, but this one was dark black. I'd never seen anything like this before, so I asked the nurse why this heart was black.

She responded with, "Oh, that's the heart of a smoker."

"Really?!" I said. "I thought smoking affected your lungs, not your heart."

Securing another electrode on my dad, she replied, "Smoking turns your insides black." This blew me away; I couldn't believe what I was seeing! I thought of my mom's side of the family, where just about everyone smokes. Then I thought of all the second-hand smoke I've breathed in throughout my life.

While the nurse finished preparing my father for his stress test, the doctor entered and quickly checked all the wires to make sure everything was hooked up properly. Then, he started the treadmill. My father took small steps as the treadmill began to turn. The doctor started a slow increase in speed, although, to me, it looked like the treadmill was barely moving.

Something on the digital readout caught the doctor's attention. With a frown, he asked my father, "Are you feeling any discomfort in your chest area?" Something was clearly not good. My father weakly replied, "It hurts a little."

With a swift motion, the doctor shut down the treadmill and retrieved a nitroglycerin tablet from a cabinet. While he placed the tablet under my father's tongue, the doctor calmly but firmly told me to take my father immediately to the emergency room. He instructed me to get a wheelchair and not let him walk. Now, *my* heart was beating fast.

The hospital wasn't far. As I drove us to the emergency room, I prayed the whole way to God that everything would be all right. Pulling up to the emergency room, I grabbed a wheelchair, helped Dad into it, and whisked him into the hospital.

The doctor's office had called ahead, and a group of medical professionals was already waiting to take my dad back to be examined. In what seemed like a whirlwind blur of events, my father had a heart catheterization. But even after that, the doctors returned to our family later that afternoon, to let us know that the catheterization was not enough to help my dad. With great heaviness, we learned that my dad had to have immediate open-heart surgery to survive.

The news was shocking to all of us. As usual, I stayed strong outwardly to support my family, but inside, I was a wreck. I love my dad dearly, and I didn't want to lose him. So, like I always tell people to do when they don't know what to do, I prayed!

The next morning was difficult. During the surgery, the doctor's discovered that my father had additional blockages in his circulatory system. After grueling hours of work, the surgeons completed six bypasses, and my father was still alive. Praise God! But he was only 49.

Seeing what my father had to endure through this surgery and afterward was a major wake up call to me to change my lifestyle choices. I made a decision then that I would be different and not allow my health to suffer because of unhealthy eating and lack of exercise. I don't want to cause my wife or children the same kind of stress I experienced that day at the hospital.

So, how's your health? Do you eat healthy food options? Do you exercise regularly? If you're like most Americans, you'd probably answer "no" to both of those questions. Did you know that according to the CDC, eliminating poor diet, inactivity, and smoking would prevent **80%** of heart disease and stroke, **80%** of type 2 diabetes, and **40%** of cancer? Those numbers are astounding!

If we are going to live better, we have to develop self-control. Would you agree that the person you struggle with saying "no" to the most is yourself? An overwhelming majority of us struggle with self-control, especially when it comes to our bodies. That tells us that most of our physical challenges are *self-imposed*. Consider what Proverbs 25:28 (NLT) says:

A person without self-control is like a city with broken-down walls.

My biggest problem is *me*, and your biggest problem is *you*. The key ingredients to any success we hope to have in this life are self-control and self-discipline. And here's how to develop them!

How to Have More Self-Control

1) Admit I have a problem.

God can't even help you with a problem you won't admit that you have. (Read that again!)

> When tempted, no one should say, "God is tempting me." For God cannot be tempted by evil, nor does he tempt anyone; but each one is tempted when, by his own evil desire, he is dragged away and enticed. James 1:13-14 (NIV)

Let me assure you that the Devil didn't make you do it. We often casually overlook or blatantly ignore our problems. We deny our problems or blame others for our problems. At SCC, we follow this saying, "Fix the problem, not the blame." The first weapon of dealing with any problem is the *truth*.

Like Jesus said in John 8:32 (NIV), "The truth will set you free."

2) Avoid temptation

I've always heard that if you don't want to be stung, stay away from bees. Rick Warren, the pastor of Saddleback Church, encourages teens to plan out their dates so that they can avoid temptations that will rise up when they're hanging out with nothing to do. You'll either be guided by your plans or your glands.

Having a plan helps not give the devil a foothold. Run from what you know will pull you down, whether that's people, places, or things.

If you want to lose weight, get rid of the candy, unhealthy snacks, and desserts in the pantry at home or in the drawers of your desk at work. Bad habits will undermine exercise all the time!

And I'm not just talking about sexual temptations and food cravings here. Many Americans are also addicted to *impulse spending*. If you can't control your credit card, cut it up or put it in a bucket of water and freeze it. I'm serious!

What in your life do you need to avoid? Listen to what Jesus prayed in Matthew 6:13 (KJV):

"Lead us not into temptation, but deliver us from evil."

I share this part of the Lord's Prayer with you because when I pray this out loud on a daily basis, it amazes me how many times God has protected me from temptation. John Maxwell is known for challenging people to change their lives by changing one small thing every day. This principle is wisdom worth far more than gold! Once I started applying this idea to my life—just changing a little something every day—I've seen dramatic positive changes in my life!

Another idea I use is to keep a journal to write down daily decisions *for the next day*. This way, you've already planned to make a change, and when the next day comes, you already know what you're going to do, which greatly increases your chances that you'll *actually do it*.

Go ahead right now and pull out a piece of paper and jot down a couple of things you'll do differently today. And then continue this process for the next 21 days. You may not see much change at first, but

I promise you that if you continue doing this consistently, it will super-charge what you want to accomplish with your life.

3) Believe you can change

Self-control begins with how you think. What you *think* determines what you *believe*, and what you *believe* determines how you *behave*.

Have an ANT Problem?

Have you ever discovered ants in your house? One day, you're at home, getting a glass of water from the sink, and you suddenly notice that the counter is alive with movement! A whole army of ants has decided to invade, and they're on the hunt for your food! To get rid of the infestation, you have to track down whatever food they've found, throw it away, seal up any other food items, and spray. After you've taken down the last ant, you feel like you've won a great victory. *Tada!*

But then the next morning...they're back! Ants are extremely persistent critters, and to defeat them, we have to repeat the process over and over until they go back outside where they belong. It's a battle that we can't stop fighting until we have the victory, or our homes will be overtaken with ants.

The same is true with making changes in our lives. We have to fight ANTs! No, not the ones in the kitchen. I'm talking about "**A**utomatic **N**egative **T**houghts."

We say to ourselves things like, "I could never stop this. It's just the way I am. I'll never be able to change. I'm just a loser. I always mess everything up. There's no hope for me."

If you catch yourself saying things like this to yourself, you have an ANT problem. Can you picture yourself waking up and feeling something on your face, and when you go look in the mirror to find out what it is, there's a parade of ants marching right into your ear? That would freak me out! If that actually happened to someone, I guarantee you that they would immediately do something to get rid of those ants!

So how do we get rid of the ANT problem? We must stop the negative self-talk. I can take a pretty good guess that you don't like people who always talk down to you. With negative self-talk, you're always talking down to YOURSELF. Let me tell you, as someone who has done this to myself for most of my life, if I talked to other people the way I've talked to myself, I wouldn't have any friends.

One of Martin Luther's well-known quotes is: "You cannot keep birds from flying over your head, but you can keep them from building a nest in your hair." Stop the ANTS by replacing those negative thoughts with verses from the Bible. Paul even encourages us to do this in Romans 12:2 (NIV):

Do not conform any longer to the pattern of this world, but be transformed by the renewing of your mind. Then you will be able to test and approve what God's will is—his good, pleasing and perfect will.

To heal the ANT problem in your mind, focus on God's promises. If outdoor ants get on your clothing, you're basically stuck with just whacking them off with your hands.

My wife, Rhonda, can't stand an insect to get on her. If one approaches, she will start swatting rapidly. If it chases her, be prepared to see my wife duck and dodge and run faster than me in a marathon if she has to!

There is a way to also remove ANTs from your mind with your hands. The empowering verse Philippians 4:13 (NKJV) is what I call the "10-Finger Reminder."

I can do all things through Christ who strengthens me.

As you read that verse again, hold up a finger for every word. The goal is that, as you look at your fingers, it will remind you that you can do all things through Christ who strengthens you.

Big Wins from Small Efforts

In his book *Bod for God*, Steve Reynolds talks about how it takes a D.I.E.T. to accomplish getting yourself back to physical wellness.

Dedication
This means to do the things you need to do daily over a long period of time. You didn't get to where you are physically overnight, and you won't get where you want to be overnight. This is where you ask God for help every day to make the right, small decisions about your diet and exercise. Remember that it's those small daily steps over time that will give you the results you desire. If you lose 1 pound a week, in a year you would lose 52 pounds! So whatever you do, just keep at it. Remember the children's storybook *The Tortoise and the Hare*? The tortoise always wins in the end.

Inspiration
Celebrate the small wins by talking about them like they're great wins because they *are* great wins! If you walked a quarter of a mile without

stopping, celebrate that. If you went out to eat with your coworkers and everyone had dessert, and you chose not to order a sugary treat, celebrate that. If you stop having negative thoughts about your body when you look in the mirror, celebrate that!

Exercise

Diet and exercise go together in order to maintain your changes. You're looking for a lifestyle change here. I've found it's hard to stop something without starting something else. Unfortunately, just saying that I'm going to cut back on my food intake doesn't accomplish anything. Without a plan, I just fall back into my old routines.

If you cut back on your intake of food and add walking or some other type of exercise, you will begin to think about how much you exercise, and you'll not want to undo the progress you've made with bad food choices. Remember, when you change your habits, your body will change as well over time.

Team

Build a circle of support. You need people to cheer you on and to encourage you when you feel like quitting. This is one of the reasons that I love programs like Weight Watchers or Bod for God groups. By joining a group, you put yourself in a place where other people can encourage you and build you up.

The reason some of us allow our bodies to get out of shape is that we have allowed someone to hurt us. We may have stopped eating for our health and started eating for our happiness. Being in a group is one of the best things you can do to help combat that thinking. You become like geese, flying in a "V" formation. When one gets tired, the others behind it start honking to encourage them on. You need to put yourself around people who have the same goals as you so that you can be encouraged and give encouragement. Remember, encouraging people are encouraged people. Look at what Ecclesiastes 4:9-10 (NIV) says about the power of groups:

> Two are better than one, because they have a good return for their labor: If either of them falls down, one can help the other up.

Your Year for Health!

I've seen this verse exemplified in my sister-in-law's life. Back when Rhonda and I were dating in high school, I hung out at Rhonda's house and went on camping trips with her family. I was really close to her mom, dad, and sister, Deanna. Deanna was 4 years older than Rhonda and I, which was great for me because I only had a driver's permit and could drive with Deanna in the car. Whereas Rhonda is quiet and easy-going, Deanna is adventurous. If I'd say something like, "I'd like to climb that mountain," she'd fire back, "Let's go do it!"

Along the way, she met a great guy named Ricky, and they married two years before Rhonda and me. Things seemed to be going really well for them, but a few years after they were married, Deanna began to have pains in her side. Her doctors discovered a growth in her lower abdominal area. It was a very scary time for her and Ricky as they awaited an official diagnosis.

Finally, the doctors concluded that she had *endometriosis*—a painful condition in which tissue from the uterus grows on organs outside the uterus. They recommended surgery and confidently assured Deanna that everything would be fine.

She had the surgery, and it seemed that the doctors were right. Everything was fine...at first. But then the symptoms returned, and she had to have the surgery again and again.

The uncertainty of what was going on inside her body, the multiple surgeries, and the fear of what would come in the future stressed Deanna almost to her breaking point. With waves of anxiety flooding her life, she began to experience severe panic attacks. The doctors prescribed an anxiety medication that helped her overcome the panic attacks, and things began turning around in a good way for Deanna. But unknown to her, the medication had an unexpected side effect: weight gain.

Over time, this very petite woman began to gain weight; however, in having to choose between weight gain or panic attacks, she elected to do without the panic attacks. (If you've ever experienced panic attacks, you have a good understanding of why she made that decision.)

As years passed, being overweight eventually led to other health issues. This happy-go-lucky "We can do it!" woman lost a lot of her energy. Her blood pressure skyrocketed, requiring her to take blood pressure medication. Her feet swelled each day until it was difficult to wear shoes. Walking for a long distance became a daunting challenge. Even short walks became difficult as she struggled to breathe. The side effects of the anxiety medication were slowly draining the life out of our precious Deanna.

During this time, Rhonda would often pray, pleading with God to intervene on behalf of her sister. Rhonda's parents would try to get Deanna to go for a walk with them at the park, but it seemed like nothing really motivated her anymore. She was very unhappy. She knew that she needed to change something to restore the quality of her life, but she didn't know what that *something* might be or look like.

After the Christmas of 2016, we decided to go on a family trip to Pigeon Forge, Tennessee. Rhonda's parents rented a cabin up on a little mountain outside of town with a beautiful view of the mountains and valley. As a family, we love to get together and hang out, laugh, eat, tell stories from our lives, and visit new places. As we started planning what we were going to do on our trip, we had to pair back a lot of our ideas because we couldn't just rush off on a hike, for instance, and leave Deanna back at the cabin. We felt that the purpose of a family trip was so that everyone could spend time with each other. So we made sure that Deanna would be included in everything we did.

The trip was a lot of memorable fun! One night, we decided to drive to a town to watch a live show. Everyone was excited, chattering away in the car. But as I drove, I had a thought go through my mind—and I didn't know if it was God instructing me to say something or if it was just my own mind giving me an idea. The thought was, "Tell Deanna that this is her year for health."

I hesitated in thought for a while as I continued to drive to our destination. I wondered, "Is this God talking to me?" I was scared to even bring up the topic because I love Deanna and didn't want to hurt her or her husband by sounding insensitive to her struggle with weight gain or by pronouncing some kind of false hope upon her. So in my mind, I asked, "God? Is this really You? Are You *really* wanting me to tell her that this is the year of her health?"

I was nervous. If God *was* speaking to me, I wanted to obey Him, but if it was just an idea from my mind, I didn't want to share it and ruin everyone's good time. Oh, decisions! Decisions!

God responded to my prayer with silence; so, I didn't bring anything up and kept driving.

Down the road, we were all hungry and stopped at an Arby's. After receiving our food, my daughter Katelyn sat in a booth with Rhonda's parents, and I sat with Rhonda, Deanna, and Ricky. As we nestled into our places, we asked God to bless the food and then started eating.

Suddenly, the words I'd heard in the car, hauntingly returned. "Tell her this is your year for health." As I shoved a bite of food into my mouth, I tried to dismiss the thought. But it persisted, repeating over and over. "Tell her this is your year for health."

The prompting to speak became so overwhelming that I fidgeted in my seat. Rhonda glanced at me and gave me a nudge. "Would you please be still?" she said under her breath.

I wrestled with this inner dilemma through most of the meal, until I couldn't take it anymore. Finally, I swallowed, wiped my lips with a napkin, and interjected, "Deanna, I feel like I need to tell you something."

Curious, she smiled at me and gave me a nod. "Go ahead. What's on your mind?"

I cleared my throat and firmly said, "I feel that I'm to tell you that *this is your year for health.*" There! I said it! Now, I tensed, waiting for a backlash, knowing that I had just messed up everyone's evening.

But to my surprise, she just looked at me and remarked, "I receive that."

As I returned to half-heartedly munching the last of my food, I wondered, "Is she upset with me? Did I hurt her feelings?" I couldn't read her emotions, and there was no more conversation about my statement. I sweated a little bit. Had I overstepped a line? I didn't know. Rhonda's side of the family isn't usually confrontational, so I just swallowed my pride and tried to enjoy the rest of the trip.

That February, Rhonda received a call from her mother to tell her that Deanna had gone back to Weight Watchers. She had tried it before but hadn't had good results. This time when she started, something was different.

Within a month, Deanna had lost 8 pounds. At three months, she set a goal of losing 25 pounds. Something marvelous was taking place! She began walking regularly, and at 5 months, she had lost 35 pounds— and it was at this point that people started to take notice.

She went shopping for new clothes; she found that she had more energy; and suddenly, she was enjoying life again! And get this: At the 7-month mark, *she* signed up our *whole family* for a 5k run/walk! I can't even express to you the joy I experienced in my heart as I walked that 5k with Deanna! God is awesome and can do truly miraculous things in your life if you partner with Him!

Because of her willingness to change, Deanna has become a new person. Not only has her body changed, but her personality has come alive again. She has self-confidence that she has never displayed before. I praise God for how her life has turned around!

One day, our family was all hanging out at Rhonda's parents' house. While I sat on the front porch, Deanna came up to me. With a smile on her face, she said to me, "Jeff, I'll never forget those words you said to me that day at the Arby's in Pigeon Forge: 'This is your year for health.' They are what motivated me to take this journey.'"

All I can say after that is, "With God all things are possible!"

My friend, if I could give you a word from God, something to really think on and put in your heart, it's:

This is your year for health!

159

Start your journey to a healthier you today! Don't wait for a diagnosis of diabetes, high blood pressure, heart disease, or cancer to try to get motivated to live healthier. If you start making healthy changes in your lifestyle now, your chances of ***avoiding*** these diseases are very high!

God is giving you an *opportunity for a better life.*

What are you going to do with it?

Chapter 10

Sharing Life Makes You Better

*B*efore I close this book, I'd like to share with you the story behind the phrase, "Opportunity for a Better Life."

In 1998, I had been the pastor of what is now called Stockbridge Community Church for 4 years. Our church had grown from 80 people to 180. We had recently relocated our church to a small building in Rex, Georgia. On the outside, things seemed to be going well for me and the church.

I had just turned 30, but something in my life wasn't right. I remember getting up on a Monday morning at 6 a.m., like I do most days, to pray and read God's Word. That morning, as I knelt to pray, I felt emotionally shaken, irritated, confused. Part of me felt spiritually dead. As I began mouthing my prayer, I heard myself say to God, "I *don't* want to do this anymore. I *don't* want to be a pastor!"

Part of my frustrations at the time revolved around having to constantly act as a mediator between warring church members. For whatever reason, they felt like the church parking lot should be where they hashed out their personal issues with each other. I'd joke with Rhonda that God called me to preach His Word, not to be a firefighter. But on this morning, the situation was no laughing matter. I was in a deep valley of decision. Something needed to change, or I was going to leave my calling.

As I prayed, I was suddenly overwhelmed with waves of sorrow. Emotions that I had bottled up trying to be a "perfect pastor" exploded inside of me, and I started crying. I lowered myself to the ground, tears falling from my face, and I growled at God, "I'm TIRED of this! If all there is to being a pastor is being a referee between people, I'm DONE!"

My body shook as I poured out my heart to God. I felt finished, done in, no longer fit to lead a church. Exasperated, I swore, "God, if You don't show me something TODAY, I'm going to resign from this church, sell my house, and move back to be with my family...because I don't know what to do. I DON'T KNOW WHAT TO DO!"

Silence.

Still weeping, I waited for an answer. "Where are You, God?" I wondered. "Did You hear me?"

More silence.

After a while, I rose to my feet with a heavy sigh. I interpreted God's silence to mean that I was on my own this time and that I needed to make my own decision. So I readied myself to tell Rhonda that it was all over and that she'd need to start packing.

Suddenly, I felt God's presence—powerful beyond imagination yet tenderly warm and loving! *I knew that His Holy Spirit was there in the room with me! I wasn't alone!*

With crystal clear detail, I saw in my mind's eye the front cover of a book that I had read a few years before! And with the image still blazing in my mind, a commanding voice instructed, "*THIS* is what I want you to do."

I was absolutely overcome! Joy, exhilaration, awe, reverence, gratitude—all washed over me like a waterfall! I could feel the darkness that had been haunting my life at that time lift off my shoulders. God hadn't just blessed me with an answer; He was also strengthening me for the challenging journey ahead.

Wiping away even more tears, I thanked God out loud and rushed over to my bookcase. Excitedly, I swept a finger across the rows and rows of book titles that stared back at me in the dim morning light. Reading the titles in my head, I discarded each of them as I hunted for the *one* that I'd seen in my mind. But I couldn't find it. Where had I put it?

I leaned forward and tilted my head, looking deeper into the recesses of my bookcase. To my delight, I discovered that I had stacked a row of books behind another row! Hastily pulling books from the shelf, my eyes finally landed on the book I sought. I picked it up and dusted off the cover while I read its title to myself: *The Purpose Driven Church*.

I opened the book, thumbing through its pages, noting passages that I had underlined when I read it some years back. I sat down at my desk and started re-reading the book. Here was God's answer, in my hands, for our church and for my future. With gratefulness, I promised, "God, I *will* do this, no matter what." I had no clue what that "no matter what" would mean and cost me in the years to come. But let me assure you that *nothing* worth achieving is ever *easy*.

Big Change Begins

I had our small staff and leadership team read *The Purpose Driven Church*. The book was a great starting point, but I felt that we needed to learn more. So, I took a handful of our staff to California to visit Saddleback Church for the "Purpose Driven Conference" with Pastor Rick Warren. Listening to speaker after speaker, one thing became extremely clear: Our church had to change its culture of thinking only about the people *inside* its walls.

Somewhere along the way, our church had taken on a "club" mentality. Though it troubles me to admit it, our church really only focused on the people inside the church. We basically ignored the rest of the community *outside* the church. We would say things like, "We need to win people to Jesus," but in reality, we mostly just came to church, had a service, and went home. After the conference, I emphasized to our staff and leaders that we needed to begin inviting people from the outside *into* our church.

Rhonda and I believe that we must live whatever we ask our church to do. So we began to build a relationship with one of our neighbors. He was a single man who had no family in the U.S. After having him over to our house a few times for dinner, we invited him to our church. Not being a Christ-follower, he gave us a lot of insight on how the "outside" world views church—and much of it was not very pleasant. But my neighbor taught me much about viewing church from a different perspective.

At this time, my son Tyler was in the 2nd grade and had become best friends with a boy named Robby Frisone. Robby wanted Tyler to spend the night one weekend, but Rhonda and I were a bit hesitant because we didn't know Robby's parents. To get to know them, Rhonda and I invited them over to our house for dinner.

Emily—a lively woman in her late 40s, who sported short, spiked hair and a rat tail in the back—was Robby's mother. Robby's father, Robert, was in his 60s and spoke in a strong New Jersey accent. Emily was a free spirit if there ever was one. She was easy going and would do anything to have fun. There was not a bit of shyness in her at all.

Later in the school year, Robby and Tyler were going on a field trip to Tybee Island, located near Savannah, Georgia. Because it was an overnight trip, the teacher needed adult chaperones, so Rhonda signed me up. Emily also signed up to chaperone the trip.

After a long bus ride, we finally arrived at the island and helped the kids settle into their rooms. I was in Robby and Tyler's room when Emily showed up with a bunch of Robby's things. Dumping his stuff on his bed, Emily wagged a finger at Robby and reminded him, "If you run out of underwear, son, just turn the ones you are wearing inside out!" I burst out with a deep laugh. I wasn't expecting her to say that.

The day went on with planned activities in different areas of the island. By bedtime, the boys in my room were getting ready to sleep, when all of a sudden, the room door flew open! Emily burst in and headed straight for Robby. I scrambled to cover myself with my shirt, while the other male chaperone, hastily snatched up his pants. Emily waved uninterestingly at us and joked, "Don't worry boys; I've seen it all!—Robby, did you find your toothbrush?" Emily loved her son.

Early in getting to know Robert and Emily, Rhonda and I knew that they were *good* people, just not Christ-followers. One time, Robert told us, "I don't like people! I do all I can to stay away from people!" Robert came across as being grumpy and blunt, but to him, he was just telling it as he saw it. And he was going to let you know what he thought about something whether you wanted to hear it or not!

After returning from one dinner with them, I turned to Rhonda and sighed, "I don't know how this is going or how to reach them. What do you think we should do?"

Rhonda kindheartedly replied, "I think we should pray for their salvation and show them love."

And that's what we did.

The friendship of our boys continued, and as time went on, they were together almost every weekend. We would take Robby on vacations with us and invited him to anything our family did. Our relationship with Robert and Emily continued to grow. We invited Robert and Emily to church whenever we felt prompted by God to bring up the topic, but they would honestly answer us that they weren't interested. Robert responded one time with, "I don't like people! Church isn't for me." Another time, Emily laughed at the invitation and added, "I'm no choir girl, Jeff! I'm not interested."

After a while, their invitation rejections wore me down. I felt like I was somehow messing this up. Rhonda and I had both centered our lives on Jesus' words in Matthew 5:14-16 (NIV):

"You are the light of the world. A city on a hill cannot be hidden. Neither do people light a lamp and put it under a bowl. Instead they put it on its stand, and it gives light to everyone in the house. In the same way, let your light shine before men, that they may see your good deeds and praise your Father in heaven."

Rhonda and I learned to love Robert and Emily dearly, and we continued to show them the love of God. Then I had a breakthrough in my thinking! I realized that this whole time, *I* was trying to save them, but I can't save them. Only God can save people. It is our responsibility as Christ-followers to love people and to let the Holy Spirit draw them to God.

All of this time, our church was in the middle of a building program. During the 2-year transition, we met in a middle school while our new facility was being built. On Easter weekend, our church held an Easter musical which Rhonda produced and would sing in. Something clicked in my mind, and I understood that this could be a golden opportunity to invite Robert and Emily one more time. Both of them loved Rhonda.

So I tried inviting them one more time. I told Robert, "Look, I understand if you don't want to come to hear me preach a sermon, but come hear Rhonda sing. She's got a great voice!" Robert thought about it for a moment and grumbled, "I'll think about it." I was surprised when Emily called us later to inform us that they *would* attend church with us if we would agree to come to their house for lunch after church. I practically dropped the phone when I heard this! "Of course, we will!" I enthusiastically agreed.

That Easter, they came to our church service at the school, and our family went to their house for lunch. Sitting around the table that day, I watched and listened for any signs of a spiritual breakthrough in their lives. They did say how much they enjoyed the musical Rhonda led and complimented her singing. I sat on the edge of my seat, hoping for an opportunity to talk about Jesus, but every time I tried to lead the conversation down that path, Robert would shut it down. I did muster up enough courage to invite them back to church with us the next week, but they both quickly told me that they didn't fit into the "church world."

I was disappointed, but I felt that something special had taken place that day. Our relationship with the Frisones had grown deeper.

In June of that year, our new church building had its final inspection, and we were all looking forward to our first Sunday service on Father's Day 2003. Our church's journey had been daunting and filled with unexpected setbacks. But now, with the building complete, we challenged our congregation to invite their friends and family to come celebrate the opening of our new building. Guess who I was going to invite.

When Emily dropped off Robby at our house for the weekend, I asked her to come to our Grand Opening. For once, she didn't seem resistant to the idea. She replied that she wouldn't say "yes" without Robert's input. There was hope!

Dropping off Robby at their house that weekend, I introduced the idea of attending our Grand Opening to Robert. I waited for his usual and direct "NO," but something extraordinary happened! Robert smiled and said, "Yeah, we'll be there to celebrate the opening of your new church." I couldn't believe it! I was expecting rejection, but God had already been long at work in the background.

On Father's Day, we opened our new church. When I went up on stage to speak, I scanned the audience, recognizing many faces and also seeing many that I didn't know. And then my eyes caught the faces of Robert and Emily sitting off toward the back of the auditorium. My heart leaped with joy! Rhonda and I were steering our church in a whole new direction, and here were the first-fruits!

After the church service, we thanked Robert and Emily for being there. They both said that they enjoyed the service. I believed beyond any doubt that God was at work in their lives.

Amazing Transformation

The next weekend rolled around with our boys spending time together, so we saw Robert and Emily as we normally did. But to our surprise, they showed up again at church the next Sunday! And *again* the following Sunday!

After they had been attending for about 6 weeks without missing a Sunday, something incredible happened! *Emily gave her life to Jesus and asked to be baptized.* I will never forget her baptism. When she went down into the water, and I brought her back up, something in her changed. She immediately threw her hands up into the air, rejoicing, and then grabbed me in a hug and kissed me on the right cheek, right there in front of the whole crowd!

I was amazed by the work God did in Emily after her baptism. Her life started changing from that day forward. It wasn't long before Robert followed and gave his life to Jesus as well. They went through our membership process to join the church, and they began to serve. Robert served as our IT tech, and Emily used her vibrant personality to greet people at the door. She loved people and had found a place to give that love away. Rhonda and I watched both of them grow in their relationship with God, and we'd say to each other, "Would you look at God!"

After three months of their newfound faith, Robert and Emily requested a private conversation with Rhonda and me after church. When we met, Robert revealed, "We need you to pray for us. Emily has had an exam for her company's insurance, and the doctor found spots on her lungs." The room became very quiet.

Emily spoke up, "I'm not worried about it, because I lived in Ohio when I was growing up, and it's common for people in that part of the state to have this. It's because of the poor air quality in the region during the time I lived there." We prayed as we all awaited the test results.

Finally, Emily heard back from the doctor...But the news was bad. She was given a diagnosis that none of us want: stage 4 lung cancer. I couldn't believe it. When I heard the news, I was just overwhelmed in shock. Emily, on the other hand, was full of faith and willing to do whatever she needed to do to get better. She had a son in middle school who she loved dearly, and she was determined to beat this disease. And so, her fight with cancer began.

Emily started a regimen of chemotherapy treatments, and those treatments took her hair, but they couldn't take her new faith in God or her love for life. She came to church on Sundays with her head uncovered, proud and strong in her determination to live. Emily had a track record of not missing a Sunday since she'd given her life to Jesus, and you can bet she wasn't going to let something like cancer break her perfect attendance!

Despite her enthusiastic personality, the cancer treatments started taking a bigger toll on her physically. Her energy level dropped really low, but that never stopped her from being the best mother she could be. Robby had a school trip to Disney World, and Emily was determined to go on this school trip as she had always done. And she went! When people would ask if she was okay, she would respond with, "I'm having the time of my life!"

Two years after her diagnosis, Emily told me something that touched my life and has led to a great change in our church. She was just waiting at church while her son was in a student ministry meeting. When I saw her, I told her how much I appreciated her joyful spirit. She looked at me with tears in her eyes and said, "Jeff, you and this church have given me and my family an *opportunity for a better life.*" She smiled with a shake of her head and added, "I would take cancer all over again to have life be as good as it has been for the last two years." She continued, "My marriage is better; my son is better; my finances are better; and my soul is better."

As I write these words, my eyes are filled with tears because those words are so deep and have changed my life forever! Since then, it has become my mission and the mission of Stockbridge Community

Church to offer people an OPPORTUNITY FOR A BETTER LIFE through JESUS CHRIST.

Cancer eventually overwhelmed Emily's body, and we laid it to rest. But it did *not* take her soul or her joyful spirit. Emily Frisone's uncrushable spirit is very much alive in me and the people of SCC. I believe that she is a part of a great cloud of witnesses in heaven, cheering for us as we take on life's challenges. In the beginning, I thought that I was reaching out to Emily for God, but in reality, God used Emily to reach out to me, to give me His purpose and His vision to live out every day that I draw breath in this world.

Emily Frisone, I dedicate this book to you. May we all learn from your life and seek to give every day to the service of God, no matter what comes our way.

CPSIA information can be obtained
at www.ICGtesting.com
Printed in the USA
LVHW030924060919
630100LV00003B/3